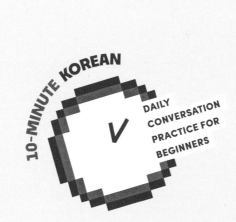

10-MINUTE KOREAN

DAILY
CONVERSATION
PRACTICE FOR
BEGINNERS

10-MINUTE KOREAN: Daily Conversation Practice For Beginners
하루 10분 한국어

1판 1쇄 · 1st edition published	2023. 9. 1.
1판 2쇄 · 2nd edition published	2024. 1. 2.

지은이 · Written by	Talk To Me In Korean
책임편집 · Edited by	선경화 Kyung-hwa Sun, 김소희 Sohee Kim
디자인 · Designed by	이은정 Eunjeong Lee, 유민지 Minji Yoo
디자인 총괄 · Designed directed by	선윤아 Yoona Sun
녹음 · Voice Recordings by	김예지 Yeji Kim, 유승완 Seung-wan Yu, 석다혜 Dahye Seok
펴낸곳 · Published by	롱테일북스 Longtail Books
펴낸이 · Publisher	이수영 Su Young Lee
편집 · Copy-edited by	강지희 Jihee Kang
주소 · Address	04033 서울특별시 마포구 양화로 113, 3층(서교동, 순홍빌딩)
	3rd Floor, 113 Yanghwa-ro, Mapo-gu, Seoul, KOREA
이메일 · E-mail	TTMIK@longtailbooks.co.kr
ISBN	979-11-91343-56-4 13710

*이 교재의 내용을 사전 허가 없이 전재하거나 복제할 경우 법적인 제재를 받게 됨을 알려 드립니다.

*잘못된 책은 구입하신 서점이나 본사에서 교환해 드립니다.

*정가는 표지에 표시되어 있습니다.

TTMIK - TALK TO ME IN KOREAN

10-MINUTE KOREAN

하루 10분 한국어

DAILY
CONVERSATION
PRACTICE FOR
BEGINNERS

Contents

Contents

PREFACE

Learning Korean is a fun experience that also requires a lot of practice, especially if you want to put it to actual use and speak it with your friends or local Korean people on your next trip to Korea. If you are looking for ways to practice Korean on a daily basis as a beginner, this book will be the best way you can spend 10 minutes each day to speak better Korean.

This book is divided into 50 chapters, and you can study one chapter each day to improve your Korean speaking skills consistently. All the vocabulary words, expressions and grammar points introduced here are beginner-friendly yet essential for daily Korean conversations.

To make sure you have a good understanding of all the key points taught in each chapter, we have included various exercises in each chapter such as Listening & Speaking Practice and Translation Practice.

Whether you have picked up this book to prepare for your next trip, to brush up on your Korean speaking, or even to start learning from the beginning, you will find yourself learning a lot and improving fast by studying with this book each day!

We hope you enjoy the book!

The book is divided into 50 small units called "Days," and you can also record the date you studied in the top left corner of this page.

DAY

01

STUDY DATE :   /

제 이름은 최경은이에요.
My name is Kyeong-eun Choi.

After you study this chapter, you will be able to introduce yourself with names, jobs, and other nouns.

Track 01

Tip
Korean surnames come before the first names.

⧗ In "Today's Conversation", you will learn simple but useful expressions that are often used in real life.

◆ ⧗ Today's Conversation

A 안녕하세요! 저는 선현우입니다.
[an-nyeong-ha-se-yo! jeo-neun seon-hyeo-nu-im-ni-da.]

반갑습니다.
[ban-gap-sseum-ni-da.]

B 네, 반가워요.
[ne, ban-ga-wo-yo.]

제 이름은 최경은이에요.
[je i-reu-meun choe-gyeong-eu-ni-e-yo.]

A Hello! I'm Hyunwoo Sun.
I'm glad to meet you.

B Yes, glad to meet you.
My name is Kyeong-eun Choi.

Listen to conversations recorded by native Korean speakers, using our mobile app TTMIK: Audio or by downloading the audio tracks on our website at https://talktomeinkorean.com/audio.

The vocabulary list provides all the major words introduced in Today's Conversation along with their English definitions.

■ **Vocabulary**
안녕하다 to be peaceful / 저 [humble] I / 반갑다 to be glad to meet / 네 yes / 제 [humble] my / 이름 name

⧗ Listening & Speaking Practice ■

Check each box after you complete each task.

✓ **Listen carefully!** Listen to the whole conversation.

Listen and repeat! Listen to each sentence one by one and

Let's role-play! Role play with the conversation.

⧗ Each conversation is played three times for you to practice listening & speaking: once to listen to the conversation at a natural pace, once to listen and repeat sentence by sentence, and once to role-play.

22   Day 01

⏳ You can study further with the Key Expression from Today's Conversation, learn the essential grammar within that expression, and also practice using various words with it.

⏳ You can practice translating what you have learned in the Key Expression to check and reinforce what you have learned.

⏳ Key Expression

저는 *　　　　　　　　　　　　이에요/예요.
[jeo-neun]　　　　　　　　　　　　[i-e-yo]/[ye-yo.]

I'm a/an _____.

* 학생　　　　student
  [hak-ssaeng]
* 회사원　　　office worker, businessman
  [hoe-sa-won]

* 선생님　　　teacher
  [seon-saeng-nim]
* 천재　　　　genius
  [cheon-jae]

Grammar Focus

• **Topic marking particles:** -은 [-eun] / -는 [-neun]

  -은 [-eun] / -는 [-neun], topic marking particles, are letting the listener know what you will talk about. You can decide whether to use -은 [-eun] or -는 [-neun] depending on the letter the previous word ends with.

  • Words ending with a final consonant → -은 [-eun]
  • Words ending with a vowel → -는 [-neun]

• **Conjugation of** -이에요 [-i-e-yo] / -예요 [-ye-yo]

  -이에요 [-i-e-yo] / -예요 [-ye-yo] means "to be" in a polite language in Korean. You can decide whether to use -이에요 [-i-e-yo] or -예요 [-ye-yo] depending on the letter the previous word ends with.

  • Words ending with a final consonant → -이에요 [-i-e-yo]
  • Words ending with a vowel → -예요 [-ye-yo]

⏳ Translation Practice

Translate the English sentences to Korean, and the Korean sentences to English, using the expression that you learned from Key Expression.

1. 저는 학생이에요.

2. I'm an office worker.

3. 저는 선생님이에요.

4. I'm a genius.

Review Quiz ■ ∙∙∙∙∙∙∙∙∙∙∙∙∙∙∙∙

[1~5] Choose the right Korean phrase from the box for the English translation.

> • 샤워하는 동안　　• 침대에 눕자마자　　• 내가 빨래할 테니까
>
> • 밤을 샜더니　　• 한국에 산 지

At the end of each of the 5 "Days," you will take a Review Quiz with 10 questions to review what you have learned in the last 5 "Days."

1. While I was showering, I danced.

   　　　　　　　　춤을 췄어요.

2. I stayed up all night and now I'm tired.

   　　　　　　　　피곤해.

3. As soon as I lay down on the bed, I fell asleep.

   　　　　　　　　잠이 들었어요.

4. I'll do the laundry, so you clean the room.

   　　　　　　　　너는 방 청소해.

5. How long have you lived in Korea?

   　　　　　　　　얼마나 됐어요?

6. Look at the picture and choose the word that matches it.

　　　빨래하다　　　　청소하다

　　　설거지하다　　　요리하다

The Korean alphabet is called 한글 [han-geul], and there are 24 basic letters and digraphs in 한글 [han-geul].
• digraph: pair of characters used to make one sound (phoneme)

Of the letters, fourteen are consonants (자음 [ja-eum]), and five of them are doubled to form the five tense consonants (쌍자음 [ssang-ja-eum]).

Consonants

Basic

ㄱ	ㄴ	ㄷ	ㄹ	ㅁ	ㅂ	ㅅ	ㅇ	ㅈ	ㅊ	ㅋ	ㅌ	ㅍ	ㅎ
g/k	n	d/t	r/l	m	b/p	s	ng	j	ch	k	t	p	h
g/k	n	d/t	r/l	m	b/p	s/ɕ	ŋ	dʑ/tɕ	tɕʰ	k/kʰ	t/tʰ	p/pʰ	h

Tense

ㄲ	ㄸ	ㅃ	ㅆ	ㅉ
kk	tt	pp	ss	jj
k'	t'	p'	s'	c'

The pronunciations of each consonant above, however, apply when the consonant is used as a beginning consonant. When those consonants are used as the final consonant of a syllable block, only seven consonants are pronounced, ㄱ, ㄴ, ㄷ, ㄹ, ㅁ, ㅂ, and ㅇ. The rest of the consonants are pronounced as one of these seven consonants when they are used as a final consonant.

- ㅋ and ㄲ are pronounced as ㄱ when they are used as a final consonant.
- ㅅ, ㅈ, ㅊ, ㅌ, ㅎ, and ㅆ are pronounced as ㄷ when they are used as a final consonant.
- ㅍ is pronounced as ㅂ when used as a final consonant.
- ㄸ, ㅃ, and ㅉ are not used as a final consonant.

When it comes to vowels (모음 [mo-eum]), there are 10 basic letters. 11 additional letters can be created by combining certain basic letters to make a total of 21 vowels. Of the vowels, eight are single pure vowels, also known as monophthongs (단모음 [dan-mo-eum]), and 13 are diphthongs (이중모음 [i-jung-mo-eum]), or two vowel sounds joined into one syllable which creates one sound.

- When saying a monophthong, you are producing one pure vowel with no tongue movement.
- When saying a diphthong, you are producing one sound by saying two vowels. Therefore, your tongue and mouth move quickly from one letter to another (glide or slide) to create a single sound.

Vowels

Monophthongs

ㅏ	ㅓ	ㅗ	ㅜ	ㅡ	ㅣ	ㅐ	ㅔ
a	eo	o	u	eu	i	ae	e
a/aː	ʌ/əː	o/oː	u/uː	ɨ/ɯː	i/iː	ɛ/ɛː	e/eː

Diphthongs

ㅑ	ㅕ	ㅛ	ㅠ		ㅒ	ㅖ
ya	yeo	yo	yu		yae	ye
ja	jʌ	jo	ju		jɛ	je

ㅘ	ㅝ		ㅙ	ㅞ
wa	wo		wae	we
wa	wʌ/wəː		wɛ	we

- ㅚ and ㅟ were pronounced as single pure vowels (monophthongs) in the past; however, presently, these vowels are produced as two vowels gradually gliding into one another to create one sound (diphthong).

ㅚ	ㅟ	ㅢ
oe	wi	ui
we	wi	ɨi

- Please refer to the book "한글마스터(Hangeul Master)" for more information.

Writing 한글 [han-geul] letters

한글 [han-geul] is written top to bottom, left to right. For example:

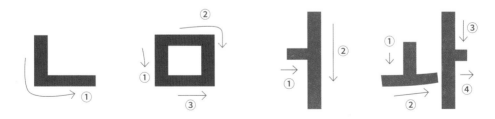

By making sure you follow the stroke order rules, you will find that writing Korean is quite easy and other people will be able to better read your handwriting.

Syllable Blocks

Each Korean syllable is written in a way that forms a block-like shape, with each letter inside the block forming a sound/syllable.

In each syllable block, there is a:

1. • Beginning consonant
2. • Middle vowel
3. Optional final consonant

• Required in a syllable block. A block MUST contain a minimum of two letters: 1 consonant and 1 vowel.

ㅊ + ㅣ + ㄴ
ch + i + n = chin

ㄱ + ㅜ
g + u = gu

친 (chin) + 구 (gu) = 친구 (chingu) = Friend

Two of the most common ways to write consonant and vowel combinations in Korean are horizontally and vertically (the boxes drawn here are for illustrative purpose only).

C   Consonant   V   Vowel

By adding a final consonant (받침 [bat-chim]), the blocks are modified:

C   Consonant   V   Vowel

There are also syllables which have two Final consonants, such as:

* In each syllable block, the letters are either compressed or stretched to keep the size relatively the same as the other letters.

Place Holder in Front of Vowels

Since the "minimum two letter" rule exists and one letter has to be a consonant and the other has to be a vowel, what can you do when a vowel needs to be written in its own syllable block? Add the consonant ㅇ [ng] in front of or on top of the vowel. When reading a vowel, such as 아 [a], the ㅇ makes no sound, and you just pronounce the ㅏ [a].

* Vowels Absolutely, Cannot, Under Any Circumstances Be Written By Themselves!!

Korean Speech Levels

In Korean, the relationship between the speaker/writer and the audience or listener is reflected in speech. It is most commonly known as "speech levels", where a speaker uses either formal or informal forms of speech to the person being spoken to, regardless of the topic being discussed.

The speech levels are determined by the verb ending.

There are three basic verb endings used to express different speech levels:

* **Type 1**   – ㅂ니다 [-m-ni-da]
  the most polite and most formal ending

* **Type 2**   – (아/어/여)요 [-(a/eo/yeo)-yo]
  the polite, natural, and slightly formal ending

* **Type 3**   – 아/어/여 [-a/eo/yeo]
  the casual, informal, and intimate ending

Types 1 and 2 fall under the honorific and polite category called 존댓말 [jon-daen-mal]
and Type 3 goes into the casual category called 반말 [ban-mal]

존댓말 [jon-daen-mal] is the honorific and polite form which is used to speak to someone who is older or in a higher societal position than you. Even when speaking to someone who is younger or in a lower societal position than you, it is polite to use 존댓말 [jon-daen-mal] until you get permission to use casual language from them.

반말 [ban-mal] is casual form which is used to speak to someone who is younger or in a lower societal position than you, someone of the same age as you, or someone you are friendly with. If you are not sure that you can use 반말 [ban-mal] to someone, you can use 존댓말 [jon-daen-mal] until you get permission to use 반말 [ban-mal] from them.

Speech Levels mainly used in this book:

존댓말 [jon-daen-mal] **with the ending -(아/어/여)요** [-(a/eo/yeo)-yo]

As a beginner, it will be safe and useful to learn 존댓말 [jon-daen-mal], so the expressions introduced in this book are mostly in 존댓말 [jon-daen-mal]. Since the ending -ㅂ니다 [-m-ni-da] is too formal to use in everyday life, the ending -(아/어/여)요 [-(a/eo/yeo)-yo] is mainly used.

-ㅂ니다 [-m-ni-da] is also used in this book, but only in formal situations or in conversations between people who have not met before. And there are some 반말 [ban-mal] expressions to help you to practice the casual form in Korean.

Basic Korean Greetings

When you say hello

Hello! / Hi!

안녕하세요?
[an-nyeong-ha-se-yo?]

- 안녕하세요 [an-nyeong-ha-se-yo] is from 안녕
하다 [an-nyeong-ha-da], which means "to be
peaceful" and you can use this expression as
"Hello".

(on the phone) Hello?

여보세요?
[yeo-bo-se-yo?]

When you meet someone for the first time

Happy to meet you.

반가워요.
[ban-ga-wo-yo.]

반갑습니다.
[ban-gap-sseum-ni-da.]

When you say goodbye

Go safely.

안녕히 가세요.
[an-nyeong-hi ga-se-yo.]

Stay safely.

안녕히 계세요.
[an-nyeong-hi gye-se-yo.]

See you next time.

다음에 봐요.
[da-eu-me bwa-yo.]

See you tomorrow.

내일 봐요.
[nae-il bwa-yo.]

When you go to sleep

Sleep well.

잘 자요.
[jal ja-yo.]

안녕히 주무세요.
[an-nyeong-hi ju-mu-se-yo.]

When you are thankful

Thank you.

* If someone thanks you, you can answer with 네 [ne] which means "Okay", or 아니에요 [a-ni-e-yo] which means "It was nothing" in this context.

고마워요.
[go-ma-wo-yo.]

고맙습니다.
[go-map-sseum-ni-da.]

감사합니다.
[gam-sa-ham-ni-da.]

When you are sorry

I am sorry.

* If someone says sorry to you, you can answer with 괜찮아요 [gwaen-cha-na-yo], which means "It is okay" or "I am okay".

미안해요.
[mi-an-hae-yo.]

죄송합니다.
[joe-song-ham-ni-da.]

When you want to excuse yourself

One moment, please.

잠시만요.
[jam-si-man-yo.]

I'm sorry, but...

죄송한데요.
[joe-song-han-de-yo.]

When you have a meal

I'll enjoy this meal.
(before you eat)

잘 먹겠습니다.
[jal meok-kket-sseum-ni-da.]

I have enjoyed this meal.
(after you eat)

잘 먹었습니다.
[jal meo-geot-sseum-ni-da.]

When you celebrate

Congratulations!

축하해요!
[chu-ka-hae-yo!]

축하합니다!
[chu-ka-ham-ni-da!]

Happy birthday!

생일 축하해요!
[saeng-il chu-ka-hae-yo!]

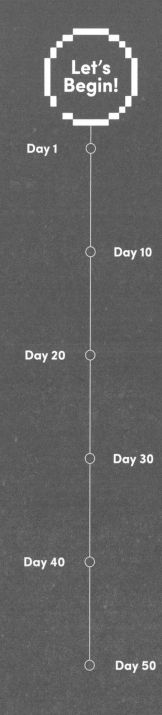

Let's
Begin!

Day 1

Day 10

Day 20

Day 30

Day 40

Day 50

01

제 이름은 최경은이에요.
My name is Kyeong-eun Choi.

After you study this chapter, you will be able to introduce yourself with names, jobs, and other nouns.

Track 01

Tip

Korean surnames come before the first names.

⏳ **Today's Conversation**

A 안녕하세요! 저는 선현우입니다.
[an-nyeong-ha-se-yo! jeo-neun seon-hyeo-nu-im-ni-da.]
반갑습니다.
[ban-gap-sseum-ni-da.]

B 네, 반가워요.
[ne, ban-ga-wo-yo.]
제 이름은 최경은이에요.
[je i-reu-meun choe-gyeong-eu-ni-e-yo.]

A Hello! I'm Hyunwoo Sun.
I'm glad to meet you.

B Yes, glad to meet you.
My name is Kyeong-eun Choi.

Vocabulary ....

안녕하다 to be peaceful / 저 [humble] I / 반갑다 to be glad to meet / 네 yes / 제 [humble] my / 이름 name

⏳ **Listening & Speaking Practice**

Check each box
after you complete
each task.

✓	**Listen carefully!** Listen to the whole conversation.
	Listen and repeat! Listen to each sentence one by one and repeat.
	Let's role-play! Role play with the conversation.

저는 •

[jeo-neun]

이에요/예요.

[i-e-yo]/[ye-yo.]

I'm a/an _____ .

• 학생   student
[hak-ssaeng]

• 선생님   teacher
[seon-saeng-nim]

• 회사원   office worker, businessman
[hoe-sa-won]

• 천재   genius
[cheon-jae]

Grammar Focus

• **Topic marking particles:** -은 [-eun] / -는 [-neun]

-은 [-eun] / -는 [-neun], topic marking particles, are letting the listener know what you will talk about. You can decide whether to use -은 [-eun] or -는 [-neun] depending on the letter the previous word ends with.

  • Words ending with a final consonant → -은 [-eun]

  • Words ending with a vowel → -는 [-neun]

• **Conjugation of** -이에요 [-i-e-yo] / -예요 [-ye-yo]

-이에요 [-i-e-yo] / -예요 [-ye-yo] means "to be" in a polite language in Korean. You can decide whether to use -이에요 [-i-e-yo] or -예요 [-ye-yo] depending on the letter the previous word ends with.

  • Words ending with a final consonant → -이에요 [-i-e-yo]

  • Words ending with a vowel → -예요 [-ye-yo]

⧗ Translation Practice

Translate the English sentences to Korean, and the Korean sentences to English, using the expression that you learned from Key Expression.

1. 저는 학생이에요.

2. I'm an office worker.

3. 저는 선생님이에요.

4. I'm a genius.

STUDY DATE :   /

저 학생 아니에요.
I'm not a student.

After you study this chapter, you will be able to express the indefinite form of a noun.

Track 02

Tip
아니에요 [a-ni-e-yo]
means "it is not",
"I am not", "you are
not", "he/she is not",
but 아니요 [a-ni-yo]
means just "No." and
both can be used in
polite situations.

⌛ Today's Conversation

A 현우 씨는 학생이에요?
[Hyeo-nu ssi-neun hak-ssaeng-i-e-yo?]

B 저 학생 아니에요.
[jeo hak-ssaeng a-ni-e-yo.]

A 아, 선생님이에요?
[ah, seon-saeng-ni-mi-e-yo?]

B 아니요, 저는 학부모예요.
[a-ni-yo, jeo-neun hak-ppu-mo-ye-yo.]

A   Hyunwoo, are you a student?

B   I'm not a student.

A   Oh, are you a teacher?

B   No, I'm a parent of a student.

Vocabulary

씨 Mr., Mrs., Ms. / 학생 student / 저 [humble] I / 아 ah / 선생님 [honorific] teacher / 아니 no / 학부모 parent of a student

⌛ Listening & Speaking Practice

Listen carefully! Listen to the whole conversation.
Listen and repeat! Listen to each sentence one by one and repeat.
Let's role-play! Role play with the conversation.

저(는) •

[jeo(neun)]

(이/가) 아니에요.

[(i/ga) a-ni-e-yo.]

I'm not a/an _____.

• **한국 사람** [han-guk ssa-ram]	Korean person	• **청소년** [cheong-so-nyeon]	teenager
• **연예인** [yeo-nye-in]	celebrity	• **바보** [ba-bo]	fool

Grammar Focus

• **Subject marking particles: -이 [-i] / -가 [-ga]**

-이 [-i] / -가 [-ga] are subject marking particles, so you can let the listener know that the word in front of -이 [-i] / -가 [-ga] is the subject of the sentence. You decide whether to use -이 [-i] or -가 [-ga] depending on the letter the previous word ends with.

  • Words ending with a final consonant → -이 [-i]
  • Words ending with a vowel → -가 [-ga]

• **Leaving out the particles**

Korean speakers often leave out the particles in the sentences when they talk. If you use particles fully, it would be "저는 학생이 아니에요. [jeo-neun hak-saeng-i a-ni-e-yo.]" instead of "저 학생 아니에요. [jeo hak-saeng a-ni-e-yo.]"

⌛ **Translation Practice**

Translate the English sentences to Korean, and the Korean sentences to English, using the expression that you learned from Key Expression.

1. I'm not a Korean person.

2. I'm not a celebrity.

3. 저는 청소년이 아니에요.

4. 저는 바보가 아니에요.

이게 뭐예요?

What's this?

After you study this chapter, you will be able to ask and answer about something.

Tip

If you want to say a word simply but in an honorific way, you can just add -(이)요 [-(i)yo] after the word like 떡볶이요 [tteok-ppo-kki-yo] or 김밥이 요 [gip-ppa-bi-yo].

⏳ Today's Conversation

A 이게 뭐예요?
[i-ge mwo-ye-yo?]

B 떡볶이요. 한국 음식이에요.
[tteok-ppo-kki-yo. han-guk eum-si-gi-ye-yo.]

A 저거는 뭐예요?
[jeo-geo-neun mwo-ye-yo?]

B 그건 김밥이에요.
[geu-geon gim-ppa-bi-e-yo.]

A What's this?

B Tteokbokki. It's Korean food.

A What's that?

B It's gimbap.

Vocabulary

이거 this thing / 뭐 what / 떡볶이 stir-fried rice cake / 한국 Korea, Korean / 음식 food / 저 거 that thing / 그거 it, the thing / 김밥 seaweed rice roll

⏳ Listening & Speaking Practice

Listen carefully! Listen to the whole conversation.	
Listen and repeat! Listen to each sentence one by one and repeat.	
Let's role-play! Role play with the conversation.	

⧗ Key Expression

•

이/가 뭐예요?
[i/ga mwo-ye-yo?]

What is _____?

• **이름**   name
  [i-reum]

• **전공**   major (in college)
  [jeon-gong]

• **직업**   job, occupation
  [ji-geop]

• **취미**   hobby
  [chwi-mi]

Grammar Focus

• **this, that, and it in Korean**

The words for "this", "that", and "it" change their forms depending on whether they are pronouns or adjectives. As adjectives, you put 이 [i], 저 [geo], 그 [geu] before the noun. As pronouns, you put 거 [geo] after them, like 이거 [i-geo], 저거 [jeo-geo], 그거 [geu-geo].

이 [i]	this (near you)	저 [jeo]	that (over there)	그 [geu]	the / that (near the other person)
이거 [i-geo]	this thing	저거 [jeo-geo]	that thing	그거 [geu-geo]	it / the thing / that thing

• **Shortening the pronouns and particles**

When 이거 [i-geo], 저거 [jeo-geo], 그거 [geu-geo] comes with particles, you can shorten them.

ex:
  • 이거 [i-geo] + -이/-가 [-i]/[-ga] = 이게 [i-gae]
  • 이거 [i-geo] + -은/-는 [-eun]/[-neun] = 이건 [i-geon]

⧗ Translation Practice

Translate the English sentences to Korean, and the Korean sentences to English, using the expression that you learned from Key Expression.

1. What is (your) name?

2. What is (your) job?

3. 전공이 뭐예요?

4. 취미가 뭐예요?

04

저 집에 가요.

I go home. / I'm going home.

After you study this chapter, you will be able to tell where you go in the present tense.

Track 04

Tip

Korean speakers often say 파이팅 [pa-i-ting] or 화이팅 [hwa-i-ting] to cheer on someone else, which is a word that comes from the English word "fighting".

⏳ **Today's Conversation**

A 현우 씨, 어디 가요?
[hyeo-nu ssi, eo-di ga-yo?]

B 저 집에 가요. 경은 씨는 어디 가요?
[jeo ji-be ga-yo. gyeong-eun ssi-neun eo-di ga-yo?]

A 저는 화장실 가요.
[jeo-neun hwa-jang-sil ga-yo.]

B 아… 파이팅!
[a... pa-i-ting!]

A Hyunwoo, where are you going?

B I'm going home. Where are you going, Kyeong-eun?

A I'm going to the restroom.

B Ah... Good luck!

Vocabulary

씨 Mr., Mrs., Ms. / 어디 where / 가다 to go / 저 [humble] I / 집 home, house / 화장실 restroom / 아 ah / 파이팅 good luck, go for it

⏳ **Listening & Speaking Practice**

Listen carefully! Listen to the whole conversation.
Listen and repeat! Listen to each sentence one by one and repeat.
Let's role-play! Role play with the conversation.

⌛ Key Expression

저(는) • (에) 가요.
[jeo(-neun)] [(e) ga-yo.]

I go to / I'm going to _____.

- **학교** school
  [hak-kkyo]
- **사무실** office
  [sa-mu-sil]
- **강의실** lecture room
  [gang-ui-sil]
- **편의점** convenience store
  [pyeo-nui-jeom]

Grammar Focus

- **Conjugating the verbs with -아요 [-a-yo]**

  If you want to use verbs in polite way with present tense, you should conjugate verbs with -아요 [-a-yo]. First, you should drop -다 [-da] from the original verb. For example, If you want to conjugate the verb 가다 [ga-da] in polite way with present tense, it would be 가요 [ga-yo].

- **Location marking particle -에 [-e]**

  -에 [-e] is a location marking particle here, but it is not only used to mark locations. It means "at", "to" and so on, and it can be used to mark a location, a time, a situation, and many other things. In this conversation, it is used as a location marker. And as previously noted, Korean speakers often omit the particles like 저는 화장실(에) 가요. [jeo-neun hwa-jang-sil(-e) ga-yo.]

⌛ Translation Practice

Translate the English sentences to Korean, and the Korean sentences to English, using the expression that you learned from Key Expression.

1. 저 학교 가요.

2. I go to the lecture room.

3. 저는 사무실에 가요.

4. I'm going to the convenience store.

STUDY DATE :   /

책 읽어요.

I read a book. / I'm reading a book.

After you study this chapter, you will be able to tell what you do in the present tense.

Track 05

⏳ Today's Conversation

A 경은 씨, 뭐 해요?
[gyeong-eun ssi, mwo hae-yo?]

B 책 읽어요.
[chaek il-geo-yo.]

A 그 책 재미있어요?
[geu chaek jae-mi-i-sseo-yo?]

B 아니요, 재미없어요.
[a-ni-yo, jae-mi-eop-sseo-yo.]

A   Kyeong-eun, what are you doing?

B   I'm reading a book.

A   Is the book interesting?

B   No, it's not interesting.

Vocabulary

씨 Mr., Mrs., Ms. / 뭐 what / 하다 to do / 책 book / 읽다 to read / 그 that / 재미있다 to be interesting, to be fun / 아니 no / 재미없다 to be not interesting, to be not fun

⏳ Listening & Speaking Practice

Listen carefully! Listen to the whole conversation.
Listen and repeat! Listen to each sentence one by one and repeat.
Let's role-play! Role play with the conversation.

⌛ Key Expression

(저는) • 아요/어요.
[(jeo-neun)] [a-yo/eo-yo.]

I [do] _____. / I'm [doing] _____.

- 영화(를) 보다   to watch a movie
  [yeong-hwa(reul) bo-da]

- 밥(을) 먹다   to have(eat) a meal
  [bab(eul) meok-dda]

- 물(을) 마시다   to drink water
  [mul(eul) ma-si-da]

- 편지(를) 쓰다   to write a letter
  [pyeon-ji(reul) sseu-da]

Grammar Focus

- **Conjugating the verbs with** -아요 [-a-yo] / -어요 [-eo-yo] / -여요 [-yeo-yo]

  To conjugate the verbs in polite way with present tense, you can use -아요 [-a-yo] / -어요 [-eo-yo] / -여요 [-yeo-yo] with the verb stem, depending on the last letter of the verb stem.

  - If the verb stem ends with ㅏ [a] or ㅗ [o] → -아요 [-a-yo]
  - If the verb stem does NOT end with ㅏ [a] or ㅗ [o] → -어요 [-eo-yo]
  - If the verb stem is 하- [ha-] → -여요 [-yeo-yo] (하여요 [ha-yeo-yo] is usually shortened as 해요 [hae-yo].)

- **Object marking particle** -을 [-eul] / -를 [-reul]

  -을 [-eul] / -를 [-reul] is an object marking particle, it means the word in front of -을 [-eul] / -를 [-reul] is an object of the verb in the sentence. You decide whether to use -을 [-eul] / -를 [-reul] depending on the letter the previous word ends with.

  - Words ending with a final consonant → -을 [-eul]
  - Words ending with a vowel → -를 [-reul]

⌛ Translation Practice

Translate the English sentences to Korean, and the Korean sentences to English, using the expression that you learned from Key Expression.

1. I watch a movie. / I'm watching a movie.

2. I have a meal. / I'm having a meal.

3. 물 마셔요.

4. 편지 써요.

Review Quiz

[1~5] Choose the right Korean word from the box for the English translation.

• 학생	• 이름	• 물	• 편의점	• 한국 사람

1. I'm a student.

   저는 _____ 이에요.

2. I'm not Korean.

   저는 _____ 이 아니에요.

3. What's (your) name?

   _____ 이 뭐예요?

4. I go to the convenience store.

   저는 _____ 에 가요.

5. I drink water.

   저는 _____ 을 마셔요.

6. Choose the words that can be matched to "먹어요" on the left.

먹어요	○ 떡볶이	○ 한국	○ 영화
	○ 이름	○ 김밥	○ 별명

7. Choose the pairs of words that are opposites.

천재 – 바보   회사원 – 직업   학생 – 선생님   밥 – 물

8. Look at the picture and write the words to complete the sentence.

저는 책을   .

9. Write the letter that will be common in the blanks.

화장   강의   사무

10. Choose the pair which is **not** matched properly.

영화 – 보다   편지 – 먹다   물 – 마시다

STUDY DATE :   /

저는 스물네 살이에요.

I'm 24 years old.

After you study this chapter, you will be able to count numbers in native-Korean number system and tell how old you are.

Track 06

Tip

Tip

Korean speakers normally ask each other about age because there are some situations where you choose how to engage with others depending on age.

⧗ Today's Conversation

A 현우 씨는 몇 살이에요?
[hyeo-nu ssi-neun myeot ssa-ri-e-yo?]

B 저는 스물네 살이에요.
[jeo-neun seu-mul-ne sa-ri-e-yo.]

A 에이, 거짓말!
[e-i, geo-jin-mal!]

B 미안해요. 사실 서른 살이에요.
[mi-an-hae-yo. sa-sil seo-reun sa-ri-e-yo.]

A How old are you, Hyunwoo?

B I'm 24 years old.

A Hmph, that's a lie!

B Sorry. Actually I'm 30 years old.

Vocabulary

씨 Mr., Mrs., Ms. / 몇 how many / 살 age, years / 저 [humble] I / 스물넷 twenty-four / 에이 hmph, pff / 거짓말 lie / 미안하다 to be sorry / 사실 actually, in fact / 서른 thirty

⧗ Listening & Speaking Practice

Listen carefully!	Listen to the whole conversation.
Listen and repeat!	Listen to each sentence one by one and repeat.
Let's role-play!	Role play with the conversation.

저는 • 살이에요.
[jeo(neun)] [sa-ri-e-yo.]

I'm _____ years old.

* 열일곱   seventeen   * 서른둘   thirty-two
  [yeol-il-gop]   [seo-reun-dul]

* 스물셋   twenty-three   * 서른아홉   thirty-nine
  [seu-mul-set]   [seo-reun-a-hop]

Grammar Focus

· **Native-Korean numbers & Sino-Korean numbers**

There are two systems of numbers in Korean: native-Korean numbers and sino-Korean numbers, and you use different numeration systems depending on the categories like age, date, time, money.

· **For age: Native-Korean numbers? Sino-Korean numbers?**

There are two ways of saying your age, but the way with "native-Korean numbers" is used more in ordinary and everyday usage. Sino-Korean numbers are used to express your age only in very formal settings. In ordinary usage, you can just put 살 [sal] after the native Korean number.

** You can find the numeration tables on page 154.

⏳ Translation Practice

Translate the English sentences to Korean, and the Korean sentences to English, using the expression that you learned from Key Expression. Write down the age in Hangeul, not numbers.

1. I'm seventeen years old.

2. I'm twenty-three years old.

3. 저 서른두 살이에요.

4. 저는 서른아홉 살이에요.

오늘 5월 22일이에요.

Today is May 22nd.

After you study this chapter, you will be able to count numbers in Sino-Korean and you can talk about the dates and days.

Track 07

Tip

If you want to say the date and the day together, you can put the date first and then the day, like 5월 22일 월요일 [o-wol i-si-bi-il wo-ryo-il].

⏳ Today's Conversation

A 오늘이 몇 월 며칠이에요?
[o-neu-ri myeot wol myeo-chi-ri-e-yo?]

B 오늘 5월 22일이에요.
[o-neul o-wol i-si-bi-i-ri-e-yo.]

A 고마워요. 아, 무슨 요일이에요?
[go-ma-wo-yo. a, mu-seun yo-i-ri-e-yo?]

B 하하, 월요일요!
[ha-ha, wo-ryo-il-yo!]

A What date is it today?

B Today is May 22nd.

A Thank you. Oh, what day is it?

B Haha, it's Monday!

Vocabulary

오늘 today / 몇 how many, what number / 월 month / 며칠 what date / 일 day / 고맙다 to be thankful / 아 ah / 무슨 what, what kind of / 요일 day of the week / 하하 haha / 월요일 Monday

⏳ Listening & Speaking Practice

Listen carefully! Listen to the whole conversation.
Listen and repeat! Listen to each sentence one by one and repeat.
Let's role-play! Role play with the conversation.

오늘(은) •
[o-neul(eun)]

월 •
[wol]

일이에요.
[i-ri-e-yo.]

Today is _____.

* **3월 1일**
  [sa-mwol i-ril]

  March 1st

* **8월 15일**
  [pa-rwol si-bo-il]

  August 15th

* **5월 8일**
  [o-wol pa-ril]

  May 8th

* **12월 31일**
  [si-bi-wol sam-si-bi-ril]

  December 31st

Grammar Focus

• **For date: Sino-Korean Number system**

In Korean, the names for the 12 months in a year are very simple. Just add the word 월 [wol], which means "month", after the Sino-Korean number. You can also simply say days in a month by adding the Sino-Korean number to the Korean word 일 [il], which means "day".

** You can find the numeration tables for date on page 158.

• **The days of the week**

Korean words for the days of the week have roots in Chinese characters. Each day has the meaning that relates to a creature in nature.

** You can find the "Days of the Week" tables on page 159.

⧗ Translation Practice

Translate the English sentences to Korean, and the Korean sentences to English, using the expression that you learned from Key Expression. Write down the date in Hangeul, not numbers.

1. 오늘(은) 삼월 일 일이에요.

2. Today is May 8th.

3. Today is August 15th.

4. 오늘(은) 십이월 삼십일 일이에요.

08

생일이 언제예요?

When is your birthday?

After you study this chapter, you will be able to ask and answer what date the special days are.

⏳ Today's Conversation

A 경은 씨, 생일이 언제예요?

[gyeong-eun ssi, saeng-i-ri eon-je-ye-yo?]

B 2월 13일요.

[i-wol sip-ssa-mil-yo.]

A … 제 생일은 안 물어봐요?

[... je saeng-i-reun an mu-reo-bwa-yo?]

B 안 궁금해요.

[an gung-geu-mae-yo.]

A Kyeong-eun, when is your birthday?

B It's February 13th.

A ... You don't ask about my birthday?

B I'm not curious.

Vocabulary

씨 Mr., Mrs., Ms. / 생일 birthday / 언제 when / 월 month / 일 day / 제 [humble] my / 안 not / 물어보다 to ask / 궁금하다 to be curious

⏳ Listening & Speaking Practice

Listen carefully! Listen to the whole conversation.
Listen and repeat! Listen to each sentence one by one and repeat.
Let's role-play! Role play with the conversation.

•

(이/가) 언제예요?
[(i/ga) eon-je-ye-yo?]

When is _____?

* 시험
  [si-heom]

exam, test

* 휴가
  [hyu-ga]

vacation

* 결혼식
  [geol-hon-sik]

wedding ceremony

* 월급날
  [wol-geum-nal]

payday

Grammar Focus

· **The expressions to ask the date of certain days**

When you want to ask the date of certain days, you can use -이/가 몇 월 며칠이에요? [-i/ga myeot wol myeo-chi-ri-e-yo?] as you learned in the previous chapter. Also, you can use -이/가 언제예요? [-i/ga eon-je-ye-yo?], which is a simpler way to say the same thing. It basically means "When is the day?".

⧖ Translation Practice

Translate the English sentences to Korean, and the Korean sentences to English, using the expression that you learned from Key Expression.

1. 시험이 언제예요?

2. When is the wedding ceremony?

3. When is the vacation?

4. When is payday?

STUDY DATE :   /

7시 30분이에요.
It's 7:30.

After you study this chapter, you will be able to ask and answer about the time with both numeration systems in Korean.

Track 09

Tip

Instead of 일곱 시 삼십 분이에요. [il-gop-ssi sam-sip-bbu-ni-e-yo.], you can also say 일곱 시 반이에요. [il-gop-ssi ba-ni-e-yo]. 반 [ban] means "half" in Korean.

⌛ Today's Conversation

A 지금 몇 시예요?
[ji-geum myeot ssi-ye-yo?]

B 7시 30분이에요.
[il-gop-ssi sam-sip-ppu-ni-e-yo.]

A 영화 언제 시작해요?
[yeong-hwa eon-je si-ja-kae-yo?]

B 8시에 시작해요. 빨리 와요!
[yeo-deol-ssi-e si-ja-kae-yo. ppal-li wa-yo!]

A What time is it now?

B It's 7:30.

A When does the movie start?

B It starts at 8. Come quickly!

Vocabulary

지금 now / 몇 how many, what number / 시 hour / 분 minute / 영화 movie / 언제 when / 시작하다 to start / 빨리 quickly / 오다 to come

⌛ Listening & Speaking Practice

Listen carefully! Listen to the whole conversation.
Listen and repeat! Listen to each sentence one by one and repeat.
Let's role-play! Role play with the conversation.

●

시 · 분이에요.

[si]　　　　　　　　[bu-ni-e-yo.]

It's _____ : _____.

● 하나 [hana]	one	● 일 [il]	one
● 셋 [set]	three	● 십 [sip]	ten
● 다섯 [da-seot]	five	● 이십오 [i-si-bo]	twenty-five
● 여덟 [yeo-deol]	eight	● 오십구 [o-sip-kku]	fifty-nine

Grammar Focus

· **For time: Both number systems are used together!**

You say "hours" in native-Korean numbers, and "minutes" in sino-Korean numbers.

You should use both number systems at the same time. It helps you to distinguish which one is referring to hours or minutes in speaking situations.

** You can find the numeration tables for time on page 156.

⌛ Translation Practice

Translate the English sentences to Korean, and the Korean sentences to English, using the expression that you learned from Key Expression. Write down the date in Hangeul, not numbers.

1. It's 1:01.

2. It's 3:10.

3. It's 5:25.

4. 여덟 시 오십구 분이에요.

10

그거는 4만 8천 원이에요.

That one is 48,000 won.

After you study this chapter, you will be able to ask and answer about the price of the products.

Track 10

Tip

If you want to get attention, you can use 저기요 [jeo-gi-yo] which means "Hello, there", and also 여기요 [yeo-gi-yo] which means "Here, please."

⧗ Today's Conversation

A   ## 저기요. 이 바지 얼마예요?
[jeo-gi-yo. i ba-ji eol-ma-ye-yo?]

B   ## 3만 원이요.
[sam-man wo-ni-yo.]

A   ## 저 치마는 얼마예요?
[jeo chi-ma-neun eol-ma-ye-yo?]

B   ## 그거는 4만 8천 원이에요.
[geu-geo-neun sa-man pal-cheon wo-ni-ye-yo.]

A   Excuse me. How much are these pants?

B   It's 30,000 won.

A   How much is that skirt?

B   That one is 48,000 won.

Vocabulary

저기 there / 이 this / 바지 pants / 얼마 how much / 만 ten thousand / 원 won(Korean currency unit) / 저 that / 치마 skirt / 그거 it, the thing, that (thing) / 천 thousand

⧗ Listening & Speaking Practice

Listen carefully! Listen to the whole conversation.
Listen and repeat! Listen to each sentence one by one and repeat.
Let's role-play! Role play with the conversation.

그거(는) • 원이에요.
[geu-geo(neun)]   [wo-ni-ye-yo.]

That one is _____ won.

• 사천오백 [sa-cheo-no-baek]	4,500		• 십사만 구천 [sip-ssa-man gu-cheon]	149,000
• 삼만 삼천 [sam-man sam-cheon]	33,000		• 삼백만 [sam-baeng-man]	3,000,000

Grammar Focus

• **For price: Sino-Korean Number system**

If you want to say a price, just say the number and then add a 원 [won] which is the unit of measure for Korean currency. You will usually use numbers from 100 to 1,000,000 to say a price in daily life if you live in Korea.

** You can find the numeration tables on page 154.

⌛ Translation Practice

Translate the English sentences to Korean, and the Korean sentences to English, using the expression that you learned from Key Expression. Write down the amount of the money in Hangeul, not numbers.

1. 그거는 사천오백 원이에요.

2. That one is 33,000 won.

3. That one is 149,000 won.

4. 그거 삼백만 원이에요.

Review Quiz

[1~5] Choose the right Korean word from the box for the English translation.

• 열일곱	• 삼월 일 일	• 시험	• 사천오백
• 월급날	• 결혼식	• 휴가	• 세 시 십 분

1. I'm 17 years old.

   저는 ＿＿＿＿＿＿＿＿＿＿ 살이에요.

2. Today is March 1st.

   오늘은 ＿＿＿＿＿＿＿＿＿＿ 이에요.

3. When is payday?

   ＿＿＿＿＿＿＿＿＿＿ 이 언제예요?

4. It's 3:10.

   ＿＿＿＿＿＿＿＿＿＿ 이에요.

5. That one is 4,500 won.

   그거는 ＿＿＿＿＿＿＿＿＿＿ 원이에요.

6. Choose the pairs of words which have the same meaning.

   ○ 서른 – 삼십   ○ 하나 – 이   ○ 다섯 – 오   ○ 여덟 – 팔

7. Look at the picture of the clock and fill in the blank in Hangeul.

시   분이에요.

8. Look at the picture and write the words to complete the sentence.

이 언제예요?

9. According to the English translation, fill in the blank with the Korean words.

Today is Monday, May 22nd.

= 오늘은 5월 22일(오월 이십이 일)   이에요.

10. Choose the appropriate answer for the question below.

A: 영화 언제 시작해요?

B:

사만 팔천 원이에요.   여덟 시요.   스물네 살이에요.

11

한강 공원에서 운동해요.

I exercise at Han River Park.

After you study this chapter, you will be able to talk about what you do and where you do that.

Track 11

Tip

Korean speakers often omit the particles, but you can use them to emphasize or give some strong nuance.

⏳ Today's Conversation

Ⓐ 경은 씨는 아침에 뭐 해요?

Ⓑ 저 요즘 운동해요.

Ⓐ 경은 씨가 운동을 해요?

Ⓑ 네, 한강 공원에서 운동해요.

A   Kyeong-eun, what do you do in the morning?

B   I exercise these days.

A   You, Kyeong-eun, you exercise?

B   Yes, I exercise at Han River Park.

Vocabulary

씨 Mr., Mrs., Ms. / 아침 morning / 뭐 what / 하다 to do / 저 [humble] I / 요즘 these days / 운동하다 to exercise / 운동 exercise / 네 yes / 한강 Han River / 공원 park

⏳ Listening & Speaking Practice

Listen carefully! Listen to the whole conversation.
Listen and repeat! Listen to each sentence one by one and repeat.
Let's role-play! Role play with the conversation.

·

에서 ° (을/를) 해요.

In/at _____ , I [do] .

· 도서관	library	· 공부	study
· 카페	cafe	· 데이트	date, going on a date
· 사무실	office	· 일	work
· 공원	park	· 산책	taking a walk

Grammar Focus

· **Time marking particle -에**

Particle -에 has meaning of "at", "to" and so on, and it can be used to mark a location, a time, a situation, and many other things. In this conversation, -에 is used to mark a time.

· **Location marking particle -에 vs. -에서**

Location marking particle -에 expresses a location where something "is" or "exists", or a direction that you are going toward like 집에 가요, which means "I'm going (toward) home". On the other hand, -에서 expresses a location where an action is taking place like 집에서 일해요, which means "I work at home".

⧗ Translation Practice

Translate the English sentences to Korean, and the Korean sentences to English, using the expression that you learned from Key Expression.

1. 도서관에서 공부해요.

2. 카페에서 데이트해요.

3. In the office, I work.

4. At the park, I take a walk.

STUDY DATE :   /

우리 같이 저녁 먹을까요?
Shall we have dinner together?

After you study this chapter, you will be able to propose something to others.

Track 12

⏳ Today's Conversation

A 아, 너무 배고파요.

B 저도요. 우리 같이 저녁 먹을까요?

A 네! 뭐 먹을까요? 치킨?

B 좋아요!

A   Ah, I'm so hungry.

B   Me, too. Shall we have dinner together?

A   Okay! What shall we eat? Chicken?

B   Sounds good!

Vocabulary

아 ah / 너무 too much / 배고프다 to be hungry / 저 [humble] I / 우리 we / 같이 together / 저녁 evening, dinner / 먹다 to eat / 네 yes / 뭐 what / 치킨 chicken / 좋다 to be good

⏳ Listening & Speaking Practice

Listen carefully! Listen to the whole conversation.
Listen and repeat! Listen to each sentence one by one and repeat.
Let's role-play! Role play with the conversation.

우리 같이 [•]   (으)ㄹ까요?

Shall we _____ together?

- 운동하다   to exercise
- 산책하다   to take a walk
- 영화(를) 보다   to watch a movie
- 커피(를) 마시다   to drink coffee

Grammar Focus

· Particle -도

-도 is used to represent the meaning of "also" and "too". In English, the placement of the words "also" and "too" varies depending on the speaker. In Korean, however, -도 is treated as a particle and always follows the noun or pronoun.

· The ending -(으)ㄹ까요?

There are many usages of the ending -(으)ㄹ까요?, and in this conversation, it has the meaning of "suggesting doing something together". You can decide how to conjugate -(으)ㄹ까요? depending on the last letter of the verb stems.

- Verb stems ending with a consonant → -을까요?
- Verb stems ending with a vowel → -ㄹ까요?

· To conjugate -아/어/여요 with a verb stem ending with the vowel ㅡ

When you conjugate -아/어/여요 with a verb that ends with the vowel ㅡ, the vowel ㅡ will be gone. In this case, you should see the last letter in the second syllable block of the verb stem and decide which ending to conjugate among -아/어/여요. For example, in 배고프다, the last letter in the second syllable block has ㅗ, so you should use -아요.

⏳ Translation Practice

Translate the English sentences to Korean, and the Korean sentences to English, using the expression that you learned from Key Expression.

1. Shall we exercise together?

2. 우리 같이 산책할까요?

3. Shall we watch a movie together?

4. 우리 같이 커피 마실까요?

13

현우 씨도 맥주 마실래요?

Hyunwoo, do you want to drink some beer, too?

After you study this chapter, you will be able to talk about your intention or will to do something.

Track 13

⏳ **Today's Conversation**

A 현우 씨도 맥주 마실래요?

B 저는 괜찮아요. 안 마실래요.

A 왜 안 마셔요?

B 술을 잘 못 마셔요.

A Hyunwoo, do you want to drink some beer, too?

B I'm okay. I won't drink.

A Why don't you drink?

B I cannot drink alcohol well.

Vocabulary

씨 Mr., Mrs., Ms. / 맥주 beer / 마시다 to drink / 저 [humble] I / 괜찮다 to be okay / 안 not / 왜 why / 술 alcohol / 잘 well / 못 cannot

⏳ **Listening & Speaking Practice**

Listen carefully! Listen to the whole conversation.
Listen and repeat! Listen to each sentence one by one and repeat.
Let's role-play! Role play with the conversation.

•

(으)ㄹ래요?

Do you want to _____?

- 집에 가다   to go home
- 집에서 쉬다   to get some rest at home
- 빵(을) 먹다   to eat bread
- 택시(를) 타다   to take a taxi

Grammar Focus

· **The ending -(으)ㄹ래요**

The ending -(으)ㄹ래요 is used when expressing the intention or the will to do something. If you place a question mark at the end of the sentence, you can ask about someone else's intention or will. You can decide how to conjugate -(으)ㄹ래요 depending on the last letter of the verb stems.

- Verb stems ending with a consonant + -을래요
- Verb stems ending with a vowel + -ㄹ래요

· **The difference between 안 and 못**

안 and 못 are both adverbs and you can use it to add negative meanings to the verbs by putting them right before the verbs. 안 means "not", so you can use it when you did/do/will not do something. On the other hand, 못 means "cannot", so you can use it when you cannot do something, like 술을 못 마셔요.

⧗ Translation Practice

Translate the English sentences to Korean, and the Korean sentences to English, using the expression that you learned from Key Expression.

1. Do you want to go home?

2. 집에서 쉴래요?

3. Do you want to eat bread?

4. 택시 탈래요?

STUDY DATE :   /

우리 카페 가자.

Let's go to the cafe.

After you study this chapter, you will be able to suggest something to do in casual language.

Track 14

Tip

This whole conversation is in casual language.

Tip

Korean speakers often use 그래 or 그래요 as "Okay" or "Let's do so", to express they agree with something.

⏳ Today's Conversation

A 우리 카페 가자.

B 그래! 뭐 마실래?

A 나는 카페라떼 마실래.

B 그러면 나는 아메리카노.

A   Let's go to the cafe.

B   Okay! What do you want to drink?

A   I want to drink a cafe latte.

B   Then I'll have an americano.

Vocabulary ....

우리 we, us / 카페 cafe / 가다 to go / 그래 okay / 뭐 what / 마시다 to drink / 나 I / 카페라떼 cafe latte / 그러면 then / 아메리카노 americano

⏳ Listening & Speaking Practice

Listen carefully! Listen to the whole conversation.
Listen and repeat! Listen to each sentence one by one and repeat.
Let's role-play! Role play with the conversation.

우리 • 자.

Let's _____.

- 여행(을) 가다   to go on a trip
- 이사하다   to move to another home
- 사귀다   to date, to become a couple
- 헤어지다   to break up

Grammar Focus

· **Making a suggestion in casual language**

Normally, you can just drop the ending -요 to change formal language to casual language. To make a suggestion in formal language, you can use -(으)ㄹ까요? that we learned from Day 12, so you can use -(으)ㄹ까? to suggest something to others. But If you want to say exactly "Let's" in casual language, you should use the different verb ending, -자. You can just put -자 after the verb stem you want to say, like 하자(let's do), 먹자(let's eat).

⧖ Translation Practice

Translate the English sentences to Korean, and the Korean sentences to English, using the expression that you learned from Key Expression.

1. 우리 여행 가자.

2. Let's move to another home.

3. Let's become a couple.

4. 우리 헤어지자.

STUDY DATE :   /

여기 우유 있어요?

Is there any milk here?

After you study this chapter, you will be able to talk about whether something exists or not.

Track 15

⧖ Today's Conversation

A 사장님, 여기 우유 있어요?

B 네, 저 냉장고에 있어요.

A 감사합니다. 혹시 케이크도 있어요?

B 아니요, 케이크는 없어요.

A   Sir, is there any milk here?

B   Yes, it's in the refrigerator there.

A   Thank you. By any chance, is there any cake?

B   No, there is no cake.

Vocabulary

사장 boss / 님 [honorific] Mr., Mrs., Ms. / 우유 milk / 있다 to exist, to be / 네 yes / 저 that / 냉장고 refrigerator / 감사하다 to be thankful / 혹시 by any chance / 케이크 cake / 아니 no / 없다 to not exist, to not be

⧖ Listening & Speaking Practice

Listen carefully! Listen to the whole conversation.	
Listen and repeat! Listen to each sentence one by one and repeat.	
Let's role-play! Role play with the conversation.	

여기 [•]   (이/가) 있어요?

Is there any _____ here?

- 휴지   tissue
- 비누   soap
- 치약   toothpaste
- 수건   towel

Grammar Focus

• **Descriptive verbs 있다 and 없다**

있어요 comes from the verbs 있다, which means "to exist" or "to have". If you are talking about someone or something that exists in a specific place, you can use 있어요. If you are talking about something in your possession, you can also use 있어요 as a meaning of "to have". 없어요 comes from the verbs 없다, which means "to not exist" or "to not have".

⧖ **Translation Practice**

Translate the English sentences to Korean, and the Korean sentences to English, using the expression that you learned from Key Expression.

1. 여기 휴지 있어요?

2. Is there any soap here?

3. Is there any toothpaste here?

4. 여기 수건 있어요?

Review Quiz

[1~5] Choose the right Korean word from the box for the English translation.

• 커피	• 도서관	• 택시	• 휴지	• 여행

1. I study in the library.

   저는 _____ 에서 공부해요.

2. Shall we drink coffee together?

   우리 같이 _____ 마실까요?

3. Do you want to take a taxi?

   _____ 탈래요?

4. Let's go on a trip.

   우리 _____ 가자.

5. Is there any tissue here?

   여기 _____ 있어요?

6. Choose all of the edible items from the choices below.

   ○ 치킨　　○ 영화　　○ 비누　　○ 맥주

7. Look at the picture and write the words to complete the sentence.

저는 사무실에서 _____ .

8. Choose the items you **cannot** normally find in 카페.

수건   커피   케이크   치약

9. According to the English translation, fill in the blank with the Korean words.

No, there is no cake.

= 아니요, 케이크는 _____ .

10. Choose the appropriate answer for the question below.

A: 현우 씨도 맥주 마실래요?

B: 저는 괜찮아요.

너무 배고파요.   케이크는 없어요.   안 마실래요.

STUDY DATE :   /

한국어 할 수 있어요?
Can you speak Korean?

After you study this chapter, you will be able to talk about what you can do.

Track 16

Tip

Korean speakers use 와 or 우와 a lot instead of "wow".

⏳ Today's Conversation

A 한국어 할 수 있어요?

B 네, 할 수 있어요.

A 와! 한국어 잘해요?

B 아니요, 조금밖에 못해요.

A   Can you speak Korean?

B   Yes, I can speak it.

A   Wow! Are you good at Korean?

B   No, I can only speak a little.

Vocabulary
한국어 Korean language / 하다 to do / 네 yes / 와 wow / 잘하다 to be good at / 아니 no / 조금 a little / 못하다 to be not good at

⏳ Listening & Speaking Practice

Listen carefully!	Listen to the whole conversation.
Listen and repeat!	Listen to each sentence one by one and repeat.
Let's role-play!	Role play with the conversation.

●

(으)ㄹ 수 있어요?

Can you _____?

* 수영하다   to swim
* 운전하다   to drive
* 한글(을) 읽다   to read Hangeul
* 떡볶이(를) 만들다   to make stir-fried rice cake

Grammar Focus

· **Particle -밖에**

-밖에 is a particle which has a meaning of "only". It is usually used with a negative verb. If you say 한국어 조금밖에 못 해요, it literally means "I cannot speak Korean only a little". If you want to say "only" with other verbs which are not negative, you can use -만.

· **The meaning of -(으)ㄹ 수 있다/없다**

-(으)ㄹ 수 있다 basically means "can (do something)". 수 means "way" or "idea" and 있다 means "to exist" or "to be", so it literally means "There is a way to do something" and it is used as "can". On the other hand, 없다 has a totally opposite meaning with 있다, so -(으)ㄹ 수 없다 means "cannot (do something)". You can decide how to conjugate -(으)ㄹ 수 있다/없다 depending on the last letter of the verb stem.

  • Verb stems ending in a vowel + -ㄹ 수 있다/없다
  • Verb stems ending in a consonant + -을 수 있다/없다

⌛ Translation Practice

Translate the English sentences to Korean, and the Korean sentences to English, using the expression that you learned from Key Expression.

1. 수영할 수 있어요?

2. 운전할 수 있어요?

3. Can you read Hangeul?

4. Can you make tteokbokki?

17

한국 드라마 보고 있어요.
I'm watching a Korean drama.

After you study this chapter, you will be able to talk about what you are doing now.

Track 17

⏳ Today's Conversation

A 지금 뭐 하고 있어요?

B 한국 드라마 보고 있어요.

A 드라마 자주 봐요?

B 네, 거의 매일 봐요.

A   What are you doing now?

B   I'm watching a Korean drama.

A   Do you often watch dramas?

B   Yes, I watch almost every day.

Vocabulary ⋯⋯⋯⋯⋯⋯⋯⋯⋯⋯⋯⋯⋯⋯⋯⋯⋯⋯⋯⋯⋯⋯⋯⋯⋯⋯⋯⋯⋯⋯

지금 now / 뭐 what / 하다 to do / 한국 Korea, Korean / 드라마 drama / 보다 to watch, to see / 자주 often / 네 yes / 거의 almost / 매일 every day

⏳ Listening & Speaking Practice

Listen carefully! Listen to the whole conversation.
Listen and repeat! Listen to each sentence one by one and repeat.
Let's role-play! Role play with the conversation.

•

고 있어요.

I'm [doing] _____.

- * 과제(를) 하다   to do homework
- * 집(을) 청소하다   to clean (my) house
- * 노래(를) 듣다   to listen to music
- * 사진(을) 찍다   to take a photo

Grammar Focus

· **present progressive tense ending** –고 있어요

If you want to say what you or someone is doing right now, you can put –고 있다 after the verb stem. If you want to say it in an honorific way, you can put –어요 instead of –다 like –고 있어요.

However, you should know that Korean speakers also use the present tense, often to express what they are doing now. So both 먹고 있어요 or 먹어요 can mean to say "I'm eating."

· **Shorten the verb stem and ending**

When the verb stem ends with a vowel and the verb ending starts with another vowel, those two vowels are normally shortened. For example, you can see 봐요 which is a shorter version of 보아요. It naturally happened to pronounce the word faster and easier.

⌛ Translation Practice

Translate the English sentences to Korean, and the Korean sentences to English, using the expression that you learned from Key Expression.

1. 과제 하고 있어요.

2. I'm cleaning (my) house.

3. 노래 듣고 있어요.

4. I'm taking a photo.

STUDY DATE :   /

한국 노래 듣는 거예요?
Are you listening to Korean songs?

After you study this chapter, you will be able to impress the action with -는 거.

Tip

When Korean speakers are surprised about something, they usually say 어, 와, 우 와 instead of "wow" or "oh".

⌛ Today's Conversation

A 어! 한국 노래 듣는 거예요?

B 네, 저 한국 노래 진짜 많이 들어요.

A 노래 듣는 거 좋아해요?

B 네, 그런데 춤추는 걸 더 좋아해요.

A   Oh! Are you listening to Korean music?

B   Yes, I listen to a lot of Korean songs.

A   Do you like listening to music?

B   Yes, but I like dancing more.

Vocabulary

어 oh / 한국 Korea, Korean / 노래 song, music / 듣다 to listen / 네 yes / 저 [humble] I / 진짜 really / 많이 a lot / 좋아하다 to like / 그런데 but / 춤추다 to dance / 더 more

⌛ Listening & Speaking Practice

Listen carefully! Listen to the whole conversation.
Listen and repeat! Listen to each sentence one by one and repeat.
Let's role-play! Role play with the conversation.

•

는 거예요?

Is it that you _____?

- 서울에서 일하다 — to work in Seoul
- 매일 운동하다 — to work out every day
- 지금 점심(을) 먹다 — to have lunch now
- 혼자 공부하다 — to study by oneself

Grammar Focus

- **The meaning of -는 거예요**

In -는 거예요, 거 is a noun and it means "thing". And if you conjugate verb stems with the ending -는, those words can determine the nouns after it. So when you say 노래 듣는 거, it literally means "the thing that (you) listen to the songs", and it means "listening to the song" in a natural way.

If you use it with a question mark like -는 거예요?, it sounds like you are trying to check the facts. Also, you can use -는 거예요 without question mark, it sounds like you are emphasizing the verb's meaning in front of -는 거예요.

- **Conjugation of irregular ㄷ verbs**

This means that if a verb has ㄷ at the end of the verb stem, and it is followed by a suffix which starts with a vowel, the ㄷ will change into ㄹ. Some verbs follow this rule and some do not, so it will be good if you memorize words that follow this rule.

- 듣다(to listen) → 들어요/들어서   걷다(to walk) → 걸어요/걸어서   묻다(to ask) → 물어요/물어서

⏳ Translation Practice

Translate the English sentences to Korean, and the Korean sentences to English, using the expression that you learned from Key Expression.

1. 서울에서 일하는 거예요?

2. Is it that you work out every day?

3. Is it that you are having lunch now?

4. 혼자 공부하는 거예요?

19

저는 잘생긴 사람을 좋아해요.

I like handsome men.

After you study this chapter, you will be able to talk about what kind of people you like.

Track 19

⧗ **Today's Conversation**

A 경은 씨는 어떤 남자를 좋아해요?

B 저는 잘생긴 사람을 좋아해요.

A 하하, 그리고요?

B 똑똑한 사람도 좋아요.

A What kind of guys do you like, Kyeong-eun?

B I like handsome men.

A Haha, and?

B Smart men are also good.

Vocabulary

씨 Mr., Mrs., Ms. / 어떤 which, what kind of / 남자 guy / 좋아하다 to like / 저 [humble] I / 잘생기다 to be handsome / 사람 person / 하하 haha / 그리고 and / 똑똑하다 to be smart / 좋다 to be good

⧗ **Listening & Speaking Practice**

Listen carefully! Listen to the whole conversation.
Listen and repeat! Listen to each sentence one by one and repeat.
Let's role-play! Role play with the conversation.

저는 ● (으)ㄴ 사람을 좋아해요.

I like people who _____.

- 예쁘다　　　　　to be pretty
- 친절하다　　　　to be kind
- 노래(를) 잘하다　to be good at singing
- 요리(를) 잘하다　to be good at cooking

Grammar Focus

- **The ending -(으)ㄴ to change the descriptive verb to its adjective form**

    In Korean there is no actual adjective, but you can change a descriptive verb to its adjective form. If you can put -(으)ㄴ after the verb stem, and put the noun word after it. For example, there is a descriptive verb 잘생기다 which means "to be handsome", you can make it as 잘생긴 to change it to its adjective form, and use it like 잘생긴 사람 which means handsome person/people. You can decide how to conjugate -(으)ㄴ depending on the last letter of the verb stem.

    - Verb stems ending with a vowel → -ㄴ
    - Verb stems ending with a consonant → -은

⌛ Translation Practice

Translate the English sentences to Korean, and the Korean sentences to English, using the expression that you learned from Key Expression.

1. I like people who are pretty.

2. 저는 친절한 사람을 좋아해요.

3. I like people who are good at singing.

4. 저는 요리 잘하는 사람을 좋아해요.

20

STUDY DATE :   /

제가 제일 좋아하는 가수예요.

This is the singer that I like the most.

After you study this chapter, you will be able to about the things and people that you like.

🎧
Track 20

⏳ Today's Conversation

A 그건 누구 사진이에요?

B 아, 제가 제일 좋아하는 가수예요.

A 우와! 그 사람 눈이 고양이 눈 같아요.

B 맞아요. 그래서 이 가수 별명이 고양이예요.

A Whose photo is it?

B Oh, this is the singer that I like the most.

A Wow! That person's eyes look like cats' eyes.

B Right. So this singer's nickname is "Cat".

Vocabulary

그거 it, the thing / 누구(의) whose / 사진 photo / 제(저) [humble] I / 제일 the most / 좋아하다 to like / 가수 singer / 우와 wow / 사람 person / 눈 eye / 고양이 cat / 같다 to be same, to be like / 맞다 to be right, to be correct / 그래서 so / 이 this / 별명 nickname

⏳ Listening & Speaking Practice

Listen carefully! Listen to the whole conversation.	
Listen and repeat! Listen to each sentence one by one and repeat.	
Let's role-play! Role play with the conversation.	

(제가) ●   는 ●   이에요/예요.

This is the [noun] _____ that I [verb or phrase] _____ .

● 싫어하다	to hate		● 옷	clothes
● 자주 먹다	to often eat		● 음식	food
● 매일 듣다	to listen to every day		● 노래	song, music
● 가끔 가다	to go to sometimes		● 식당	restaurant

Grammar Focus

· **The ending -는 to change the action verb to its adjective form**

In Korean, you can also change the action verb to its adjective form to describe the nouns. For example, there is a word 좋아하다 which means "to like", and you can make it like 좋아하는, meaning "that (I) like". You can describe nouns with this, like 좋아하는 가수. If you want to put a subject with the verb, you can just add the subject like 제가 좋아하는 가수, which means "the singer that I like".

⌛ Translation Practice

Translate the English sentences to Korean, and the Korean sentences to English, using the expression that you learned from Key Expression.

1. These are the clothes that I hate.

2. This is the food that I often eat.

3. (제가) 매일 듣는 노래예요.

4. This is the restaurant that I sometimes go to.

Review Quiz

[1~5] Choose the right Korean word from the box for the English translation.

> • 운전   • 점심   • 요리   • 식당   • 사진

1. Can you drive?

_____ 할 수 있어요?

2. I'm taking a photo.

_____ 찍고 있어요.

3. Is it that you are having lunch now?

지금 _____ 먹는 거예요?

4. I like people who are good at cooking.

저는 _____ 를 잘하는 사람을 좋아해요.

5. This is the restaurant that I sometimes go to.

제가 가끔 가는 _____ 이에요.

6. Look at the picture and choose the word that matches it.

○ 수영하다   ○ 청소하다

○ 운전하다   ○ 친절하다

7. Choose the pairs which are matched properly.

매일 - sometimes   자주 - often

가끔 - every day   지금 - now

8. According to the English translation, fill in the blank with the Korean words.

This is the food that I often eat.

= 제가 _____ 이에요.

9. Choose the word that <u>**cannot**</u> be in the blank.

저는 _____ 사람을 좋아해요.

친절한   가끔 가는   노래 잘하는

10. Choose the appropriate phrase for the conversation below.

A: _____ 좋아해요?

B: 네, 그런데 춤추는 걸 더 좋아해요.

춤추는 거   노래 듣는 거   좋아하는 거

STUDY DATE :   /

저 남편이랑 영화 보러 가요.

I'll go watch a movie with my husband.

After you study this chapter, you will be able to talk about what you will do in the near future.

Track 21

⧗ Today's Conversation

A 이번 주말에 뭐 해요?

B 저 남편이랑 영화 보러 가요.

A 어떤 영화 보러 가요?

B 아직 몰라요.

A   What will you do this weekend?

B   I'll go watch a movie with my husband.

A   What movie are you going to watch?

B   I don't know yet.

Vocabulary

이번 this, this time / 주말 weekend / 뭐 what / 하다 to do / 저 [humble] I / 남편 husband / 영화 movie / 보다 to watch, to see / 가다 to go / 어떤 what kind of, which / 아직 yet / 모르다 to not know

⧗ Listening & Speaking Practice

Listen carefully! Listen to the whole conversation.	
Listen and repeat! Listen to each sentence one by one and repeat.	
Let's role-play! Role play with the conversation.	

⧖ Key Expression

저 ̇ (으)러 가요.

I'll go _____.

- 옷(을) 사다   to buy clothes
- 수업(을) 듣다   to attend class
- 치료(를) 받다   to get medical treatment
- 강아지랑 산책하다   to take a walk with the dog

Grammar Focus ....

• **Particle -(이)랑**

-(이)랑 means "and", so you can use it to list more than two nouns. Also, it has a meaning of "with" in -(이)랑, so you can tell who you do the action "with". In this conversation, it is used in the meaning of "with". You can decide how to use -(이)랑 by the last letter of the word in front of it.

  • The previous word ending with a vowel → -랑 / The previous word ending with a consonant → -이랑

• **Conjugation of -(으)러 가다**

-(으)러 is listed in the dictionary as a way to indicate the purpose of an action, so -(으)러 가다 is used when talking about going somewhere to do something. You can decide how to conjugate -(으)러 depending on the last letter of the verb stem.

  • Verb stems ending with a vowel → -러 / Verb stems ending with a consonant → -으러

• **Expressing future tense with present tense verbs**

In Korean, there are few ways to conjugate the verbs in future tense, but you can also use the present tense verbs. It still makes sense if the context tells you the conversation is about the future, or you use some words that can show that you are talking about the future.

⧖ Translation Practice

Translate the English sentences to Korean, and the Korean sentences to English, using the expression that you learned from Key Expression.

1. I'll go buy clothes.

2. 저 수업 들으러 가요.

3. I'll go get medical treatment.

4. 저 강아지랑 산책하러 가요.

STUDY DATE :   /

그냥 집에서 쉴 거예요.
I'll just get some rest at home.

After you study this chapter, you will be able to talk about future plans.

Track 22

⏳ Today's Conversation

A 오늘 저녁에 뭐 할 거예요?

B 그냥 집에서 쉴 거예요.

A 저랑 같이 한강 공원 갈래요?

B 오, 좋아요!

A What will you do this evening?

B I'll just get some rest at home.

A Do you want to go to Han River Park with me?

B Oh, sounds great!

Vocabulary

오늘 today / 저녁 evening / 뭐 what / 하다 to do / 그냥 just / 집 home / 쉬다 to get some rest / 저 [humble] me / 같이 together / 한강 Han River / 공원 park / 가다 to go / 오 oh / 좋다 to be good

⏳ Listening & Speaking Practice

Listen carefully! Listen to the whole conversation.
Listen and repeat! Listen to each sentence one by one and repeat.
Let's role-play! Role play with the conversation.

•

(으)ㄹ 거예요.

I'll _____.

- 화장실(을) 청소하다   to clean the restroom
- 한국어(를) 연습하다   to practice Korean
- 청바지(를) 입다   to wear jeans
- 버스(를) 타다   to take a bus

Grammar Focus

• **Conjugation of -(으)ㄹ 거예요**

-(으)ㄹ 거예요 is used to express intention or plan for a future action, or expectation for a future state. This is the most common way of making future tense sentences in Korean. You can decide how to conjugate -(으)ㄹ 거예요 depending on the last letter of the verb stem.

- Verb stems ending with a vowel → -ㄹ 거예요
- Verb stems ending with a consonant → -을 거예요
- Exception: Verb stems already ending with ㄹ → 거예요

⌛ Translation Practice

Translate the English sentences to Korean, and the Korean sentences to English, using the expression that you learned from Key Expression.

1. 화장실 청소할 거예요.

2. I'll practice Korean.

3. I'll wear jeans.

4. 버스 탈 거예요.

STUDY DATE :   /

저기요! 주문할게요.
Excuse me! I'll place an order.

After you study this chapter, you will be able to talk about the future plan.

Track 23

Tip

주세요 means "Please give me..." so you can put a noun in front of 주세요.

⧗ Today's Conversation

A   저기요! 주문할게요.

B   네, 뭐 드릴까요?

A   삼겹살 2인분이랑 된장찌개 하나 주세요.

B   알겠습니다.

A	Excuse me! I'll place an order.
B	Yes, what can I get you?
A	Pork belly for two and a bowl of soybean paste stew, please.
B	OK.

Vocabulary

저기 there / 주문하다 to order / 네 yes / 뭐 what / 드리다 [honorific] to give / 삼겹살 pork belly / -인분 serving / 된장찌개 soybean paste stew / 하나 one / 주다 to give / 알다 to know, to understand

⧗ Listening & Speaking Practice

Listen carefully! Listen to the whole conversation.	
Listen and repeat! Listen to each sentence one by one and repeat.	
Let's role-play! Role play with the conversation.	

•

(으)ㄹ게요.

I'll _____.

* 먼저 퇴근하다   to leave work first
* 다시 전화하다   to call you back
* 집에서 기다리다   to wait at home
* 내일 아침에 일찍 오다   to come early tomorrow morning

Grammar Focus

· **Conjugation of -(으)ㄹ게요**

-(으)ㄹ게요 is used when you talk about your plan in the future, but it is especially used when you change plans according to what the other person said, or check or assume what the other person thinks by saying something using this ending and seeing his/her reaction. You can decide how to conjugate -(으)ㄹ게요 depending on the last letter of the verb stem.

  · Verb stems ending with a vowel → -ㄹ게요
  · Verb stems ending with a consonant → -을게요

· **The difference between -(으)ㄹ 거예요 and -(으)ㄹ게요**

-(으)ㄹ 거예요 is used to express intention or plan for a future action, or expectation for a future state. This is not related to or affected by the reaction or the request of the other person in the conversation. -(으)ㄹ게요 focuses more on actions or decisions as a reaction to or as a result of what the other person says or thinks.

⧗ Translation Practice

Translate the English sentences to Korean, and the Korean sentences to English, using the expression that you learned from Key Expression.

1. I'll leave work first.

2. 다시 전화할게요.

3. 집에서 기다릴게요.

4. I'll come early tomorrow morning.

오늘 점심에 먹을 음식이에요.

This is the food that I'll eat for lunch today.

After you study this chapter, you will be able to explain some things about what you will do in the future with something.

Track 24

⏳ Today's Conversation

A 와! 음식이 엄청 많네요.

B 네, 오늘 점심에 먹을 음식이에요.

A 아, 점심에 친구들이랑 파티 해요?

B 아니요! 저 혼자 다 먹을 거예요.

A Wow! That's a lot of food.

B Yes, this is the food that I'll eat for lunch today.

A Oh, will you have a party with friends at lunch?

B No! I'll eat it all by myself.

Vocabulary

와 wow / 음식 food / 엄청 very / 많다 to be a lot of amount / 네 yes / 오늘 today / 점심 lunch / 먹다 to eat / 아 ah / 친구 friend / 파티 party / 하다 to do / 아니 no / 저 [humble] I / 혼자 alone, by oneself / 다 all

⏳ Listening & Speaking Practice

Listen carefully! Listen to the whole conversation.
Listen and repeat! Listen to each sentence one by one and repeat.
Let's role-play! Role play with the conversation.

(으)ㄹ   이에요/예요.

This is the [noun] _____ that I'll [verb or phrase] _____.

내일 입다	to wear tomorrow	옷	clothes	
저녁에 마시다	to drink at dinner	와인	wine	
1년 동안 살다	to live for a year	집	house	
한국에 가져가다	to bring to Korea	선물	gift	

Grammar Focus

· Making adjective form of a verb in the future tense with -(으)ㄹ

You already know that you can change the action verb in present tense to its adjective form to describe nouns. Now if you put -(으)ㄹ after the verb stem, you can also change the verb to its adjective form in the future tense. You can only use this with the action verbs, not descriptive verbs. You should decide how to conjugate -(으)ㄹ depending on the last letter of the verb stem.

· Verb stems ending with a vowel → -ㄹ
· Verb stems ending with a consonant → -을

Translation Practice

Translate the English sentences to Korean, and the Korean sentences to English, using the expression that you learned from Key Expression.

1. 내일 입을 옷이에요.

2. This is the wine that I'll drink at dinner.

3. This is the house that I'll live in for a year.

4. 한국에 가져갈 선물이에요.

STUDY DATE :   /

서울역 도착했어?

Did you arrive at Seoul Station?

After you study this chapter, you will be able to talk about what you did in the past.

Track 25

⏳ Today's Conversation

A 여보세요? 서울역 도착했어?

B 응, 방금 도착했어. 우리 어디서 만날까?

A 1번 출구로 와.

B 알았어. 거기서 봐!

A   Hello? Did you arrive at Seoul Station?

B   Yes, I just arrived. Where should we meet?

A   Come to exit 1.

B   I got it. See you there!

Vocabulary

여보세요 hello (on the phone) / 서울역 Seoul Station / 도착하다 to arrive / 응 yes / 방금 just (now) / 우리 we / 어디서 where / 만나다 to meet / 번 No. (for numbers) / 출구 exit / 오다 to come / 알다 to know / 거기 there / 보다 to see, to meet

⏳ Listening & Speaking Practice

Listen carefully! Listen to the whole conversation.	
Listen and repeat! Listen to each sentence one by one and repeat.	
Let's role-play! Role play with the conversation.	

•

았/었/였어?

Did you _____?

• 어제 김밥(을) 만들다   to make gimbap yesterday
• 오늘 학교(에) 다녀오다   to go and come back from school today
• 금요일에 친구(를) 만나다   to meet a friend on Friday
• 주말에 여행(을) 가다   to go on a trip on the weekend

Grammar Focus

· **Particle -(으)로**

There are a lot of usages of the particle -(으)로, but in this conversation it means "toward". You can decide how to use -(으)로 depending on the last letter of the verb stem.

- The previous word ending with a vowel → -로
- The previous word ending with a consonant → -으로

· **Conjugation of -았/었/였어요**

-았/었/였어요 is used to change verbs in the past tense. If you understand how to change verbs into the present tense, understanding how to change them into the past tense is just as easy. You can decide how to conjugate -았/었/였어요 depending on the last letter of the verb stem, same as you conjugate -아/어/여요.

- If the verb stem ends with ㅏ or ㅗ → -았어요
- If the verb stem does NOT end with ㅏ or ㅗ → -었어요
- If the verb stem is 하- → -였어요 (하였어요 is usually shortened as 했어요.)

⌛ Translation Practice

Translate the English sentences to Korean, and the Korean sentences to English, using the expression that you learned from Key Expression.

1. Did you make gimbap yesterday?

2. 오늘 학교 다녀왔어?

3. 금요일에 친구 만났어?

4. Did you go on a trip on the weekend?

Review Quiz

[1~5] Choose the right Korean word from the box for the English translation.

> • 집   • 치료   • 전화   • 연습   • 금요일

1. I'll go get medical treatment.

저 _____ 받으러 가요.

2. I'll practice Korean.

저 한국어 _____ 할 거예요.

3. I'll call you back.

다시 _____ 할게요.

4. This is the house that I'll live in for a year.

1년 동안 살 _____ 이에요.

5. Did you meet a friend on Friday?

_____ 에 친구 만났어?

6. Pick all the words that can be matched to the given word "입다" on the left.

입다	○ 옷	○ 버스
	○ 집	○ 청바지

7. Look at the picture and write the words to complete the sentence.

저는   하러 가요.

8. According to the English translation, fill in the blank with the Korean words.

These are the clothes that I'll wear tomorrow.

=   옷이에요.

9. Choose the pairs which are **not** matched properly.

어제 - 했어요   오늘 - 할 거예요   내일 - 할게요

어제 - 해요   오늘 - 했어요   내일 - 했어요

10. Choose the appropriate answer for the question below.

A: 이번 주말에 뭐 해요?

B: 저 남편이랑

저녁에 마실 와인이에요.   주말에 여행 갔어?   영화 보러 가요.

STUDY DATE :   /

한국어 공부하려고 왔어요.
I came here to study Korean.

After you study this chapter, you will be able to tell the intention about your action.

Track 26

⏳ Today's Conversation

A 어느 나라에서 왔어요?

B 저는 프랑스에서 왔어요.

A 여행하러 오셨어요?

B 아니요, 한국어 공부하려고 왔어요.

A   Which country did you come from?

B   I came from France.

A   Did you come here to travel?

B   No, I came here to study Korean.

Vocabulary

어느 which / 나라 country / 오다 to come / 저 [humble] I / 프랑스 France / 여행하다 to travel / 아니 no / 한국어 Korean language / 공부하다 to study

⏳ Listening & Speaking Practice

Listen carefully! Listen to the whole conversation.
Listen and repeat! Listen to each sentence one by one and repeat.
Let's role-play! Role play with the conversation.

•

(으)려고 왔어요.

I came here to _____.

- 여행하다   to travel
- 영어(를) 배우다   to learn English
- 계좌(를) 만들다   to make a bank account
- 콘서트 티켓(을) 사다   to buy a concert ticket

Grammar Focus

• **The meaning of** -(으)려고 하다

-(으)려고 하다 expresses the intention or will to do/want/try something or the state of something in the very near future. This is very useful for expressing your plan for the future, and shows the purpose of what you will do. Also, you can use -(으)려고 하다 with other verbs instead of 하다, like -(으)려고 오다 in this conversation, or you can just omit the verb and just use it as -(으)려고요. You should decide how to conjugate -(으)려고 depending on the last letter of the verb stem.

- Verb stems ending with a vowel → -려고
- Verb stems ending with a consonant → -으려고

⏳ Translation Practice

Translate the English sentences to Korean, and the Korean sentences to English, using the expression that you learned from Key Expression.

1. I came here to travel.

2. 영어 배우려고 왔어요.

3. I came here to make a bank account.

4. 콘서트 티켓 사려고 왔어요.

STUDY DATE :   /

그거 우리 본 영화 아니야?

Isn't it a movie that we watched?

After you study this chapter, you will be able to check what you think you did in the past.

Track 27

Tip

This whole conversation is in casual language.

Tip

Korean speakers usually call their partners with 자기야 as a meaning of "honey".

⧗ **Today's Conversation**

A 자기야, 우리 어떤 영화 볼까?

B 글쎄… 이 영화 어때?

A 그거 우리 본 영화 아니야?

B 뭐? 나는 안 봤어. 누구랑 봤어?

A Honey, what movie shall we watch?

B Well... How about this movie?

A Isn't it a movie that we watched?

B What? I didn't watch it. Who did you watch it with?

Vocabulary

자기 oneself / 우리 we / 어떤 what kind of, which / 영화 movie / 보다 to watch / 글쎄 well / 이 this / 어때 how about / 그거 it, the thing / 아니 not / 뭐 what / 나 I / 안 not / 누구 who

⧗ **Listening & Speaking Practice**

Listen carefully! Listen to the whole conversation.
Listen and repeat! Listen to each sentence one by one and repeat.
Let's role-play! Role play with the conversation.

그거 •   (으)ㄴ   아니야?

Isn't it the [noun] _____ that [verb or phrase] _____ (in the past)?

- 엄마가 보내다   mom sends
- 아빠가 주다   dad gives
- 할머니가 만들다   grandma makes
- 내가 쓰다   I write

- 과일   fruit
- 돈   money
- 떡   rice cake
- 편지   letter

Grammar Focus

· Making adjective form of a verb in the past tense with -(으)ㄴ

You can express the adjective form of a verb in the past tense with "verb stem + -(으)ㄴ". You can only use this with the action verbs, not descriptive verbs. You should decide how to conjugate -(으)ㄴ depending on the last letter of the verb stem.

- Verb stems ending with a vowel → -ㄴ
- Verb stems ending with a consonant → -은
- Exception: Verb stems ending with ㄹ → omit ㄹ and put -ㄴ

⧗ Translation Practice

Translate the English sentences to Korean, and the Korean sentences to English, using the expression that you learned from Key Expression.

1. 그거 엄마가 보낸 과일 아니야?

2. Isn't it the money that dad gave?

3. 그거 할머니가 만든 떡 아니야?

4. Isn't it the letter that I wrote?

28

아이스크림부터 끊는 거 어때요?

How about stop eating ice cream first?

After you study this chapter, you will be able to propose something to others.

Track 28

⧖ Today's Conversation

A 저 오늘부터 다이어트 시작했어요.

B 그런데 지금 뭐 먹는 거예요?

A 이거요? 아이스크림이요.

B … 아이스크림부터 끊는 거 어때요?

A I started my diet today.

B But what are you eating right now?

A This? It's ice cream.

B ... How about stop eating ice cream first?

Vocabulary

저 [humble] I / 오늘 today / 다이어트 diet / 시작하다 to start / 그런데 but / 지금 now / 뭐 what / 먹다 to eat / 이거 this / 아이스크림 ice cream / 끊다 to stop doing

⧖ Listening & Speaking Practice

Listen carefully! Listen to the whole conversation.
Listen and repeat! Listen to each sentence one by one and repeat.
Let's role-play! Role play with the conversation.

•

는 거 어때요?

How about [doing] _____ ?

- * 물(을) 많이 마시다   to drink a lot of water
- * 사탕(을) 그만 먹다   to stop eating candy
- * 핸드폰(을) 끄다   to turn off the cell phone
- * 팀장님한테 물어보다   to ask the manager

Grammar Focus

· **Particle -부터**

-부터 is a particle which means "from" when you talk about a starting point of something.

· **The meaning of -(으)는 거 어때요?**

You can use -(으)는 거 어때요? when you want to make suggestions and proposals. With -(으)는 거, you can make noun form of a verb in present tense, so it has a meaning of "doing something" here. When you ask -(으)는 거 어때요?, it will be the meaning of "How about doing something?". You should decide how to conjugate -(으)ㄴ 거 어때요? depending on the last letter of the verb stem.

- · Verb stems ending with a vowel → -는 거 어때요?
- · Verb stems ending with a consonant → -으는 거 어때요?
- · Exception: Verb stems ending with ㄹ → omit ㄹ and put -는 거 어때요?

⏳ **Translation Practice**

Translate the English sentences to Korean, and the Korean sentences to English, using the expression that you learned from Key Expression.

1. How about drinking a lot of water?

2. How about stop eating candy?

3. 핸드폰을 끄는 거 어때요?

4. 팀장님한테 물어보는 거 어때요?

STUDY DATE :   /

저 좀 도와주세요.

Please give me some help.

After you study this chapter, you will be able to ask others for help in a polite way.

Track 29

Tip

도와드리다 is a honorific version of 도와주다 which mean "to give help".

⌛ Today's Conversation

A 현우 씨, 저 좀 도와주세요.

B 뭐 도와드려요?

A 저 박스 좀 같이 들어 주세요.

B 음… 점심 사 주세요. 그러면 도와드릴게요.

A   Hyunwoo, please give me some help.

B   What can I do to help?

A   Please lift that box with me.

B   Umm... Please buy me lunch. Then I'll help you.

Vocabulary

씨 Mr., Mrs., Ms. / 저 [humble] I / 좀 some / 도와주다 to give help / 뭐 what / 돕다 to help / 저 that / 박스 box / 같이 together / 들다 to lift / 음 umm / 점심 lunch / 사다 to buy / 그러면 then

⌛ Listening & Speaking Practice

Listen carefully! Listen to the whole conversation.	
Listen and repeat! Listen to each sentence one by one and repeat.	
Let's role-play! Role play with the conversation.	

•

아/어/여 주세요.

Please _____ (for me).

* 문(을) 열다   to open the door
* 사진(을) 좀 찍다   to take some pictures
* 다시 전화하다   to call (me) again
* 편지를 쓰다   to write a letter

Grammar Focus

· **The meaning of -아/어/여 주다**

You already learned 주세요 has a meaning of "Please give me". 주다 is "to give" and if you put verb stems + -아/어/여 before 주다, it has a meaning that you do something for someone else. For example, if you conjugate a verb 사다 (to buy) and -아/어/여 주다, it means you buy something for someone else. When you conjugate them, you can follow same rule as you did with verb stems + -아/어/여요.

· **Conjugation of irregular ㅂ verbs**

There are some situations where the verb has ㅂ at the end of the verb stem, and the ending that you try to add starts with a vowel, like 돕다(to help) + -아/어/여요. Then ㅂ will change 오 or 우. You should change it depending on the previous letter of ㅂ.

  · If the vowel before ㅂ is 오, change ㅂ to 오.
  · If the vowel before ㅂ is NOT 오, change ㅂ to 우.

⏳ Translation Practice

Translate the English sentences to Korean, and the Korean sentences to English, using the expression that you learned from Key Expression.

1. 문 열어 주세요.   **2.** 사진 좀 찍어 주세요.

3. Please call me again.   **4.** Please write a letter.

STUDY DATE :   /

그거 예쁜데 진짜 비싸요.
That one is pretty but really expensive.

After you study this chapter, you will be able to contrast two characters of things in one sentence.

Track 30

⌛ Today's Conversation

A 경은 씨, 뭐 하고 있어요?

B 가방 사려고 인터넷에서 검색하고 있어요.

A 오, 이 가방 예쁘다. 이거 어때요?

B 그거 예쁜데 진짜 비싸요. 400만 원이에요.

A Kyeong-eun, what are you doing?

B I was searching on the internet to buy a bag.

A Oh, this bag looks cute. How about this one?

B That one is pretty but really expensive. It's 4 million won.

Vocabulary

씨 Mr., Mrs., Ms. / 뭐 what / 하다 to do / 가방 bag / 사다 to buy / 인터넷 internet / 검색하다 to search / 오 oh / 이 this / 예쁘다 to be pretty / 이거 this, this thing / 그거 the thing, that / 진짜 really / 비싸다 to be expensive / 만 ten thousand / 원 won(Korean currency unit)

⌛ Listening & Speaking Practice

Listen carefully! Listen to the whole conversation.
Listen and repeat! Listen to each sentence one by one and repeat.
Let's role-play! Role play with the conversation.

•

(으)ㄴ/는데   아/어/여요.

_____ but _____

• 강아지가 크다	The dog is big.	• 귀엽다	to be cute
• 방이 깨끗하다	The room is clean.	• 싸다	to be cheap
• 사람은 많다	There are lots of people.	• 음식은 적다	There is little food.
• 가방은 작다	The bag is small.	• 책은 크다	The book is big.

Grammar Focus

· **The conjugation of** -(으)ㄴ/는데

-(으)ㄴ/는데 has many usages, but in this conversations, it shows a result or situation which is contrasting to the previous action or situation. While the basic structure ends in -데, the words or phrases which come right before -데 change a bit.

- · After action verbs, after 있다 and 없다 → -는데
- · After descriptive verbs ending with final consonant → -은데
- · After descriptive verbs ending in a vowel or the consonant ㄹ, after 이다 and 아니다 → -ㄴ데

⧗ Translation Practice

Translate the English sentences to Korean, and the Korean sentences to English, using the expression that you learned from Key Expression.

1. 강아지가 큰데 귀여워요.

2. The room is clean but cheap.

3. 사람은 많은데 음식은 적어요.

4. The bag is small but the book is big.

Review Quiz

[1~5] Choose the right Korean phrase from the box for the English translation.

- 사진 좀 찍어
- 엄마가 보낸
- 사람은 많은데
- 계좌 만들려고
- 사탕을 그만 먹는

1. I came here to make a bank account.

   _____ 왔어요.

2. Isn't it the fruit that mom sent?

   그거 _____ 과일 아니야?

3. How about stop eating candy?

   _____ 거 어때요?

4. Please take some pictures for me.

   _____ 주세요.

5. There are lots of people but there is little food.

   _____ 음식은 적어요.

6. Choose the item which is **not** edible from the choices below.

   ○ 과일   ○ 떡   ○ 사탕   ○ 영어

7. Look at the picture and write the words to complete the sentence.

책은 커요.

8. Choose the pairs which are **not** matched properly.

사진 - 만들다   핸드폰 - 끄다   펜 - 마시다   강아지 - 귀엽다

9. According to the English translation, fill in the blank with the Korean words.

Please call me again.

=   주세요.

10. Choose the appropriate answer for the question below.

A: 여행하러 오셨어요?

B: 아니요,   왔어요.

펜 좀 빌려   한국어 공부하려고   방이 깨끗한데

STUDY DATE :   /

그 영화 보지 마세요.
Don't watch that movie.

After you study this chapter, you will be able to talk to others about what they should not do.

Track 31

Tip

Korean speakers often use 그래? or 그래요? as "Is that so?", to express they are surprised.

⏳ Today's Conversation

A 경은 씨, 이 영화 봤죠? 재미있어요?

B 아, 그 영화 보지 마세요. 진짜 재미없어요.

A 그래요? 현우 씨가 이 영화 추천해 줬어요.

B 현우 씨가 추천하는 영화는 다 재미없어요.

A Kyeong-eun, you watched this movie, right? Is it interesting?

B Ah, don't watch that movie. It's really boring.

A Is that so? Hyunwoo recommended this movie to me.

B All the movies that Hyunwoo recommends are boring.

Vocabulary
씨 Mr., Mrs., Ms. / 이 this / 영화 movie / 보다 to watch / 재미있다 to be interesting / 진짜 really / 재미없다 to be boring / 그래? Is that so? / 추천하다 to recommend / 다 all

⏳ Listening & Speaking Practice

Listen carefully! Listen to the whole conversation.
Listen and repeat! Listen to each sentence one by one and repeat.
Let's role-play! Role play with the conversation.

●

지 마세요.

Don't _____.

* 만지다   to touch
* 마시다   to drink
* 들어가다   to go in
* 가져가다   to take

Grammar Focus

• **Conjugation of** -지 마세요

-지 마세요 is made with the verb 말다 which means "to quit doing", "to not do", "to stop doing". When using -(으)세요 with 말다, it becomes 마세요. When combining 마세요 with other verbs to say "do not do" or "stop doing" something, -지 is needed after the verb stem. You can put -지 마세요 after the verb stem to say "Don't do" something.

⌛ Translation Practice

Translate the English sentences to Korean, and the Korean sentences to English, using the expression that you learned from Key Expression.

1. 만지지 마세요.

2. Don't drink.

3. Don't go in.

4. 가져가지 마세요.

32

바다에 수영하러 가고 싶어.

I want to go swimming at the beach.

After you study this chapter, you will be able to talk about what you want to do.

🎧 Track 32

Tip

This whole conversation is in casual language.

Tip

When Korean speakers use the verbs in their original form like 덥다, it expresses a nuisance when they are talking to themselves.

⏳ Today's Conversation

A 아, 너무 덥다. 바다에 수영하러 가고 싶어.

B 나도 바다 가고 싶어! 같이 갈래?

A 좋아! 언제 갈까?

B 이번 주는 시간이 안 돼. 다음 주 금요일 어때?

A Ah, it's so hot. I want to go swimming at the beach.

B I want to go to the beach, too! Want to go together?

A Sounds good! When should we go?

B I cannot make time this week. How about next Friday?

Vocabulary ··

아 ah / 너무 so, much / 덥다 to be hot / 바다 ocean, beach / 수영하다 to swim / 가다 to go / 나 I / 같이 together / 좋다 to be good / 언제 when / 이번 this time / 주 week / 시간 time / 안 not / 되다 to be able to / 다음 next / 금요일 Friday

⏳ Listening & Speaking Practice

Listen carefully! Listen to the whole conversation.	
Listen and repeat! Listen to each sentence one by one and repeat.	
Let's role-play! Role play with the conversation.	

•

고 싶어.

I want to _____.

- 집에서 나가다　　　　to leave home
- 이 영화(를) 다시 보다　　to watch this movie again
- 남자 친구(를) 사귀다　　to have a boyfriend
- 맛있는 음식(을) 먹다　　to eat delicious food

Grammar Focus

• **Conjugation of -고 싶어**

In English, you put "want to" before the verb, but in Korean, you change the ending of the verbs. You can just put -고 싶어 after the verb stem like 먹고 싶어, 하고 싶어. Also, you can simply ask someone what they want to do like 뭐 먹고 싶어? 뭐 하고 싶어?

X Translation Practice

Translate the English sentences to Korean, and the Korean sentences to English, using the expression that you learned from Key Expression.

1. I want to leave home.

2. 이 영화(를) 다시 보고 싶어.

3. I want to have a boyfriend.

4. I want to eat delicious food.

33

자전거 탈 줄 알아요?
Do you know how to ride a bike?

After you study this chapter, you will be able to talk about the things that you know how to do.

Track 33

⏳ Today's Conversation

A 현우 씨, 자전거 탈 줄 알아요?

B 네, 저 토요일마다 자전거 타러 가요. 같이 갈래요?

A 저는 자전거 탈 줄 몰라요.

B 제가 가르쳐 줄게요.

A Hyunwoo, do you know how to ride a bike?

B Yes, I go to ride my bike every Saturday. Do you want to go together?

A I don't know how to ride a bike.

B I'll teach you.

Vocabulary
씨 Mr., Mrs., Ms. / 자전거 bike / 타다 to ride / 알다 to know / 네 yes / 저 [humble] I / 토요일 Saturday / 마다 every / 가다 to go / 같이 together / 모르다 to not know / 제 [humble] I / 가르치다 to teach

⏳ Listening & Speaking Practice

Listen carefully! Listen to the whole conversation.	
Listen and repeat! Listen to each sentence one by one and repeat.	
Let's role-play! Role play with the conversation.	

•

(으)ㄹ 줄 알아요.

I know how to _____.

* 한글(을) 쓰다   to write Hangeul
* 피아노(를) 치다   to play the piano
* 불고기(를) 만들다   to cook bulgogi
* 세탁기(를) 사용하다   to use the washing machine

Grammar Focus

· **Conjugation of -(으)ㄹ 줄 알아요/몰라요**

When you are talking about "knowing how to do something" or "being able to do something", you can use -(으)ㄹ 줄 as a meaning of how/method. If you put 알아요 after that, it means "I know how to do it". Oppositely, if you put 몰라요, it means "I don't know how to do it". You should decide how to conjugate -(으)ㄹ 줄, depending on the last letter of the verb stem.

* Verb stems ending with a vowel → -ㄹ 줄
* Verb stems ending with a consonant → -을 줄
* Exception: Verb stems already ending with ㄹ → 줄

· **Conjugation of irregular 르 verbs**

This means that if a verb has 르 at the end of the verb stem, and it is followed by -아/어/여요, -아/어/여서, -았/었/였 어요, then the 르 will change "double ㄹ". However, even if the verb stem ends with -르, if it is then followed by other endings, such as -고, -는데, etc., -르 will still stay the same.

ex: 모르다 → 몰라요 / 몰라서 / 몰랐어요 / 모르고 / 모르는데 ...

⏳ Translation Practice

Translate the English sentences to Korean, and the Korean sentences to English, using the expression that you learned from Key Expression.

1. 한글 쓸 줄 알아요.

2. I know how to play the piano.

3. 불고기 만들 줄 알아요.

4. I know how to use the washing machine.

STUDY DATE :   /

저 친구랑 게임해도 돼요?

Is it okay if I play games with my friend?

After you study this chapter, you will be able to ask for permission from someone.

Track 34

Tip

In this conversation, A is talking in formal language, B is talking in casual language.

⌛ Today's Conversation

A 엄마, 저 친구랑 게임해도 돼요?

B 숙제는 다 했어?

A 아니요, 게임 먼저 하고 숙제할게요.

B 안 돼. 숙제 먼저 하고 게임해.

A   Mom, is it okay if I play games with my friend?

B   Did you finish your homework?

A   No, I'll play games first and then do my homework.

B   Nope. Finish your homework first and then play games.

Vocabulary

엄마 mom / 저 [humble] I / 친구 friend / 게임하다 to play a game / 되다 to be possible / 숙제 homework / 다 all / 아니 no / 먼저 first / 숙제하다 to do homework / 안 not

⌛ Listening & Speaking Practice

Listen carefully! Listen to the whole conversation.	
Listen and repeat! Listen to each sentence one by one and repeat.	
Let's role-play! Role play with the conversation.	

⏳ Key Expression

•

아/어/여도 돼요?

Is it okay if I _____?

- 집에 일찍 가다   to go home early
- 카페에 강아지(를) 데려가다   to bring a dog to the cafe
- 방에서 음악(을) 듣다   to listen to music in the room
- 영화관에서 햄버거(를) 먹다   to eat a hamburger in the theater

Grammar Focus

- **The meaning and conjugation of -아/어/여도 돼요?**

  Basically, 되다 means "to be okay", "to be doable", or "to be possible" and -아/어/여도 means "even if..." or "even when". So all together, -아/어/여도 되다 means "to be okay (even) if..." That is why -아/어/여도 돼요? can have the meaning for getting permission. When you conjugate them, you can follow same rule as you did with -아/어/여.

  - Verb stems ending in vowels ㅏ or ㅗ + -아도
  - Verb stems ending in other vowels + -어도
  - Verb stems ending with 하 + 여도 (It is normally be shortened as 해도.)

- **How to connect two sentences in one: -고**

  By using the verb ending -고, you can combine two sentences together. -고 has same meaning with 그리고, which means "and" or "and then" in Korean, so you can combine two sentences as one with -고. You can just put -고 after the verb stem of the first sentence, and put another verb of the second sentence, like 게임 먼저 하고 숙제할게요.

⏳ Translation Practice

Translate the English sentences to Korean, and the Korean sentences to English, using the expression that you learned from Key Expression.

1. 집에 일찍 가도 돼요?

2. Is it okay if I bring a dog to the cafe?

3. 방에서 음악 들어도 돼요?

4. Is it okay if I eat a hamburger in the theater?

35

보통 키인 것 같아요.

It seems like it's just average height.

After you study this chapter, you will be able to talk about what you think or assume.

Track 35

Tip

Korean speakers say 키가 어떻게 되세요? to ask other people's height, which literally means "How is your height done?" to ask for personal information indirectly.

Tip

Korean speakers use centimeters to measure their height, and they usually omit the word "centimeters" and just say the number only.

⏳ Today's Conversation

A 경은 씨는 키가 어떻게 되세요?

B 163이에요.

A 163이면 한국에서 키가 큰 거예요?

B 음… 제 생각에는 보통 키인 것 같아요.

A How tall are you, Kyeong-eun?

B I'm 163 (centimeters).

A Is 163 (centimeters) tall in Korea?

B Umm... It seems like it's just average height.

Vocabulary

씨 Mr., Mrs., Ms. / 키 height / 어떻다 to be how / 되다 to be / 한국 Korea / 크다 to be tall / 음 well / 제 [humble] my / 생각 thinking, opinion / 보통 normal

⏳ Listening & Speaking Practice

Listen carefully!	Listen to the whole conversation.
Listen and repeat!	Listen to each sentence one by one and repeat.
Let's role-play!	Role play with the conversation.

•

(으)ㄴ 것 같아요.

It seems like _____.

* 좋은 사람이다   He/She is a good person.
* 맛이 괜찮다   The taste is okay.
* 불이 너무 밝다   The light is too bright.
* 날씨가 조금 춥다   The weather is a bit cold.

Grammar Focus

· How to say "it seems to be" with descriptive verbs

You can use -(으)ㄴ 것 같아요 to say "it seems to be". To understand this, you should know 같다 means "it looks like" or "it seems to be", and if you put -(으)ㄴ 것 after the verb stem, so you can make the verb as its noun form. You should decide how to conjugate them depending on the last letter of the verb stem.

- · Verb stems ending with a vowel → -ㄴ 것 같아요
- · Verb stems ending with a consonant → -은 것 같아요

· How to say "it looks like" with action verbs

You can use -(으)ㄴ 것 같아요 or -는 것 같아요 to say "it looks like" with action verbs. If you want to speak in the past tense, you should say -(으)ㄴ 것 같아요 exactly same as you did with descriptive verbs. If you want to speak in the present tense, you can use -는 것 같아요.

⏳ Translation Practice

Translate the English sentences to Korean, and the Korean sentences to English, using the expression that you learned from Key Expression.

1. 좋은 사람인 것 같아요.

2. 맛이 괜찮은 것 같아요.

3. It seems like the light is too bright.

4. It seems like the weather is a bit cold.

Review Quiz

[1~5] Choose the right Korean phrase from the box for the English translation.

> • 불고기 만들 줄 　　• 집에 일찍 가도 　　• 들어가지
>
> • 남자 친구 사귀고 　　• 날씨가 조금 추운

1. Don't go in.

_____ 마세요.

2. I want to have a boyfriend.

_____ 싶어.

3. I know how to cook bulgogi.

_____ 알아요.

4. Is it okay if I go home early?

_____ 돼요?

5. It seems like the weather is a bit cold.

_____ 것 같아요.

6. Choose the pairs of words which are **not** opposites.

○ 재미있다 - 재미없다 　　○ 덥다 - 바다

○ 알다 - 모르다 　　○ 좋다 - 괜찮다

7. Look at the picture and write the words to complete the sentence.

줄 알아요.

8. Choose the pair which is __not__ matched properly.

자전거 - 타다   키 - 크다   한글 - 밝다   날씨 - 춥다

9. According to the English translation, fill in the blank with the Korean words.

Is it okay if I bring a dog to the cafe?

= 카페에 강아지 _____ 도 돼요?

10. Choose the appropriate answer for the question below.

A: 163이면 한국에서 키가 큰 거예요?

B: 음... 제 생각에는 _____

보통 키인 것 같아요.   가르쳐 줄게요.   키가 어떻게 되세요?

DAY

36

좀 기다리셔야 돼요.

You should wait a bit.

After you study this chapter, you will be able to talk to others about what they should do.

Track 36

⧖ Today's Conversation

A 사장님, 지금 자리 있어요?

B 자리가 없어요. 좀 기다리셔야 돼요.

A 얼마나 기다려야 돼요?

B 30분 정도 기다리셔야 될 것 같아요.

A   Hello, do you have empty seats now?

B   We don't have empty seats. You should wait a bit.

A   How long should we wait?

B   I think you should wait for around 30 minutes.

Vocabulary

사장 boss / 님 [honorific] Mr., Mrs., Ms. / 지금 now / 자리 seat / 있다 to exist, to be / 없다 to not exist, to be not / 좀 a little / 기다리다 to wait / 얼마 how long / 분 minute / 정도 around, about

⧖ Listening & Speaking Practice

Listen carefully! Listen to the whole conversation.
Listen and repeat! Listen to each sentence one by one and repeat.
Let's role-play! Role play with the conversation.

•

아/어/여야 돼요.

You should _____.

* 8시에 비행기(를) 타다   to get on the flight at 8 o'clock
* 1시까지 사무실에 들어가다   to go into the office by 1 o'clock
* 12시에 출발하다   to depart at 12 o'clock
* 6시까지 근무하다   to work until 6 o'clock

Grammar Focus

• **Conjugation of -아/어/여야 돼요**

If you use -아/어/여야 돼요, it takes the meaning of "should" or "to have to". 되다 means "to be done" or "to be possible", so -아/어/여야 돼요 actually means "you should do this to make things done and okay." When you conjugate them, you can follow same rule as you did with verb stems + -아/어/여.

- Verb stems ending in the vowels ㅏ or ㅗ → -아야
- Verb stems ending in other vowels → -어야
- Verb stems ending with 하 → -여야 (It is normally be shortened as 해야.)

⧗ Translation Practice

Translate the English sentences to Korean, and the Korean sentences to English, using the expression that you learned from Key Expression.

1. 8시에 비행기 타야 돼요.

2. You should go into the office by 1 o'clock.

3. You should depart at 12 o'clock.

4. 6시까지 근무해야 돼요.

37

내가 오늘 발을 안 씻어서 그래.

It's because I didn't wash my feet today.

After you study this chapter, you will be able to talk about the reason and the result of some situations.

Track 37

Tip

This whole conversation is in casual language.

Tip

You can use 귀찮아 when you are annoyed, or too lazy to do something.

⌛ Today's Conversation

A 방에서 이상한 냄새 나는 것 같아.

B 내가 오늘 발을 안 씻어서 그래. 미안해.

A 야, 가서 빨리 발 씻어. 토할 것 같아.

B 싫어. 귀찮아.

A   I think the room smells weird.

B   It's because I didn't wash my feet today. Sorry.

A   Hey, go wash your feet quickly. I feel like puking.

B   I don't want to. It's annoying.

Vocabulary

방 room / 이상하다 to be weird / 냄새나다 to smell / 나 I / 오늘 today / 발 foot / 안 not / 씻다 to wash / 미안하다 to be sorry / 야 hey / 가다 to go / 빨리 quickly / 토하다 to vomit, to puke / 싫다 to dislike / 귀찮다 to be annoyed

⌛ Listening & Speaking Practice

Listen carefully! Listen to the whole conversation.	
Listen and repeat! Listen to each sentence one by one and repeat.	
Let's role-play! Role play with the conversation.	

•

아/어/여서 그래.

It's because _____ .

* 내가 졸리다   I'm sleepy.
* 엄마가 바쁘다   Mom is busy.
* 아빠가 배고프다   Dad is hungry.
* 강아지가 심심하다   The dog is bored.

Grammar Focus

· **Conjugation of -아/어/여서**

-아/어/여서 is coming from 그래서, which means "therefore" or "so" in Korean. You can make two sentences as one by just putting -아/어/여서 after the verb stem of the first sentence, and put the second sentence after. When you conjugate them, you can follow same rule as you did with verb stems + -아/어/여.

  · Verb stems ending in vowels ㅏ or ㅗ + -아서
  · Verb stems ending in other vowels + -어서
  · Verb stems ending with 하 + 여서 (It is normally be shortened as 해서.)

· **Two different usage of -아/어/여서 in this conversation**

There are few usage of -아/어/여서, but in this conversation, it is used for two different usages. One is for reason and result. You can put the reason part before -아/어/여서, and result part after like 발을 안 씻어서 그래. The second usage is when an action and another action that takes place after the first action. You can put the first action before -아/어/여서, and next action after like 가서 발 씻어.

☒ Translation Practice

Translate the English sentences to Korean, and the Korean sentences to English,
using the expression that you learned from Key Expression.

1. 내가 졸려서 그래.

2. It's because mom is busy.

3. It's because dad is hungry.

4. 강아지가 심심해서 그래.

STUDY DATE :   /

그릇 뜨거우니까 조심하세요.

The bowl is hot, so be careful.

After you study this chapter, you will be able to talk to others about what to do and explain the reason.

Track 38

⏳ Today's Conversation

A 주문하신 음식 나왔습니다.

B 아, 여기로 주세요.

A 네, 그릇 뜨거우니까 조심하세요.

B 감사합니다.

A   The food you ordered has arrived.

B   Ah, please put it here.

A   Okay, the bowl is hot, so be careful.

B   Thank you.

Vocabulary

주문하다 to order / 음식 food / 나오다 to come out / 아 ah / 여기 here / 주다 to give / 네 yes, okay / 그릇 bowl / 뜨겁다 to be hot / 조심하다 to be careful / 감사하다 to be thankful

⏳ Listening & Speaking Practice

Listen carefully! Listen to the whole conversation.
Listen and repeat! Listen to each sentence one by one and repeat.
Let's role-play! Role play with the conversation.

•

(으)니까 조심하세요.

_____, so be careful.

- 길(이) 미끄럽다   The road is slippery.
- 가방(이) 무겁다   The bag is heavy.
- 사람(이) 엄청 많다   There are many people.
- 뒤에 차(가) 오다   The car is coming behind you.

Grammar Focus

• **Conjugation of -(으)니까**

You can use -(으)니까 to express that the verb which comes before -(으)니까 is the reason for another action or the basis of a judgment. So, you can put the first verb or phrase with -(으)니까 as the reason part, and then put the second verb or phrase after. In this conversation, the second part is 조심하세요, so you can talk to others to be careful and tell them the reason in the phrase with -(으)니까. You should decide how to conjugate -(으)니까 depending on the last letter of the verb stem.

- Verb stems ending with a vowel → -니까
- Verb stems ending with a consonant → -으니까

⌛ Translation Practice

Translate the English sentences to Korean, and the Korean sentences to English, using the expression that you learned from Key Expression.

1. The road is slippery, so be careful.

2. The bag is heavy, so be careful.

3. 사람이 엄청 많으니까 조심하세요.

4. 뒤에 차가 오니까 조심하세요.

39

어제 뛰다가 넘어졌어요.

Yesterday I was running and then fell down.

After you study this chapter, you will be able to talk about two different actions that are connected.

🎧
Track 39

Tip

In this conversation, A is talking in casual language, B is talking in formal language.

⏳ **Today's Conversation**

Ⓐ **어머, 너 팔이 왜 그래?**

Ⓑ **어제 뛰다가 넘어졌어요.**

Ⓐ **아이고! 엄청 크게 멍들었네.**

Ⓑ **네, 너무 아파요.**

A   Oh, what happened to your arm?

B   Yesterday I was running and then fell down.

A   Oh, my! You got a huge bruise.

B   Yes, it hurts so much.

Vocabulary ··

어머 oh / 너 you / 팔 arm / 왜 why / 그렇다 to be so / 어제 yesterday / 뛰다 to run / 넘어지다 to fall down / 아이고 oh, my / 엄청 very / 크다 to be big / 멍들다 to get a bruise / 네 yes / 너무 too much / 아프다 to be hurt

⏳ **Listening & Speaking Practice**

Listen carefully! Listen to the whole conversation.	
Listen and repeat! Listen to each sentence one by one and repeat.	
Let's role-play! Role play with the conversation.	

다가　　　　　　　　았/었/였어요.

I was [doing] _____ and then _____ .

• 학교에 가다	to go to school	돈을 줍다	to pick up the money
• 잠을 자다	to sleep	꿈을 꾸다	to have a dream
• 길을 건너다	to cross the street	친구를 만나다	to meet a friend
• 통화하다	to talk over the phone	잠이 들다	to fall asleep

Grammar Focus

· **Conjugation of -다가**

When you want to express things that happen during or shortly after one another, you can use the verb ending -다가. This is a commonly used verb ending in Korean when you are talking about a gradual transition from one action to another or one situation to another. It is very easy to conjugate a verb with -다가, you can just put verb stem with -다가. But make sure, when you use -다가, the subject of the sentence should be the same for both of the verbs.

⏳ **Translation Practice**

Translate the English sentences to Korean, and the Korean sentences to English, using the expression that you learned from Key Expression.

1. 학교에 가다가 돈을 주웠어요.

2. 잠을 자다가 꿈을 꿨어요.

3. I was crossing the street and then I met my friend.

4. I was talking over the phone and then I fell asleep.

40

홍대입구역에서 지하철 타시면 돼요.
You can take the subway at Hongik University Station.

After you study this chapter, you will be able to propose to others what they can do.

Track 40

⏳ Today's Conversation

A 죄송한데요. 여기서 서울역까지 어떻게 가요?

B 홍대입구역에서 지하철 타시면 돼요.

A 감사합니다. 서울역 가는 버스도 있어요?

B 네, 있어요. 그런데 버스 타면 더 오래 걸려요.

A Excuse me. How can I get to Seoul Station from here?

B You can take the subway at Hongik University Station.

A Thank you. Is there a bus to go to Seoul Station?

B Yes, there is. But it takes longer if you take a bus.

Vocabulary
죄송하다 [humble] to be sorry / 여기 here / 서울역 Seoul Station / 어떻게 how / 가다 to go / 홍대입구역 Hongik University Station / 지하철 subway / 타다 to ride / 감사하다 to be thankful / 버스 bus / 있다 to exist, to be / 네 yes / 그런데 but / 더 more / 오래 for a long time / 걸리다 to take (time)

⏳ Listening & Speaking Practice

Listen carefully! Listen to the whole conversation.	
Listen and repeat! Listen to each sentence one by one and repeat.	
Let's role-play! Role play with the conversation.	

•

(으)면 돼요.

You can _____.

- 아침 9시까지 오다   to come by 9 A.M.
- 서류(를) 제출하다   to submit the document
- 가방(을) 여기에 두다   to put the bag here
- 휴지(를) 거기서 가져가다   to take tissue from there

Grammar Focus

· Conjugation of -(으)면 돼요

In order to add the meaning "if" to a verb, add -(으)면 to the verb stem. When you say -(으)면, it means "if", and 되다 means "to be done" or "to be possible". So -(으)면 돼요 has the meaning of "It is okay if you do this".

- Verb stems ending with ㄹ or a vowel + -면 돼요
- Verb stems ending with consonants other than ㄹ + -으면 돼요

⧗ Translation Practice

Translate the English sentences to Korean, and the Korean sentences to English, using the expression that you learned from Key Expression.

1. 아침 9시까지 오면 돼요.

2. You can submit the document.

3. 가방 여기에 두면 돼요.

4. You can take tissue from there.

Review Quiz

[1~5] Choose the right Korean phrase from the box for the English translation.

> • 학교에 가다가　　　• 사무실에 들어가야　　　• 엄마가 바빠서
>
> • 뒤에 차 오니까　　　• 가방 여기에 두면

1. You should go into the office by 1 o'clock.

   1시까지 _____ 돼요.

2. It's because mom is busy.

   _____ 그래.

3. The car is coming behind you, so be careful.

   _____ 조심하세요.

4. I was going to school and then picked up the money.

   _____ 돈을 주웠어요.

5. You can put the bag here.

   _____ 돼요.

6. Choose the pair which is **not** matched properly.

   ○ 냄새 - 나다　　　○ 잠 - 자다　　　○ 지하철 - 타다　　　○ 배 - 많다

7. Look at the picture and choose the word that matches it.

돈	그릇
서류	휴지

8. Choose the word which is **not** related to a feeling.

귀찮다　　　미안하다　　　들어가다　　　감사하다

9. According to the English translation, fill in the blank with the Korean words.

I was talking over the phone and then fell asleep.

= ＿＿＿＿＿＿＿＿＿ 잠이 들었어요.

10. Choose the appropriate answer for the question below.

A: 어머, 너 팔이 왜 그래?

B:

어제 뛰다가 넘어졌어요.　　　여기로 주세요.　　　토할 것 같아.

빨리 방학 되면 좋겠다!

It would be great if vacation comes quickly!

After you study this chapter, you will be able to express your wish.

Track 41

Tip

This whole
conversation is in
casual language.

⌛ Today's Conversation

A   아, 빨리 방학 되면 좋겠다!

B   이번 방학에 무슨 계획 있어?

A   응, 나 한국 여행 가려고! 서울 갔다가 제주도 갈 거야.

B   좋겠다. 잘 다녀오고 내 선물 사 와!

A   Ah, it would be great if vacation comes quickly!

B   Do you have any plans for this vacation?

A   Yes, I'll go on a trip to Korea. I'll go to Seoul and then Jeju Island.

B   Sounds nice. Have a good trip and buy me some souvenirs!

Vocabulary

아 ah / 빨리 quickly / 방학 vacation / 되다 to become / 좋다 to be good / 이번 this time / 무슨 what kind of, any / 계획 plan / 있다 to exist, to be / 응 yes / 나 I / 한국 Korea / 여행 trip / 가다 to go / 서울 Seoul / 제주도 Jeju Island / 잘 well / 다녀오다 to go and come back / 내 my / 선물 gift / 사다 to buy / 오다 to come

⌛ Listening & Speaking Practice

Listen carefully! Listen to the whole conversation.
Listen and repeat! Listen to each sentence one by one and repeat.
Let's role-play! Role play with the conversation.

•

(으)면 좋겠다!

It would be great if _____ !

* 월급(이) 오르다   I get a raise at work.
* 빨리 토요일(이) 되다   Saturday comes quickly.
* 날씨(가) 따뜻해지다   The weather gets warmer.
* 생일 선물(을) 많이 받다   I receive a lot of birthday gifts.

Grammar Focus

• Many usages of -겠-

-겠- is a suffix that you can use when you express one's intention or assumption. -겠- has many usages, it can be used to express what you are going to do, to talk about something that will happen, to show your assumption about something, or to talk about possibilities or capabilities. -겠- needs to be used between the verb stem and verb ending.

• The meaning of -(으)면 좋겠다

-(으)면 has the meaning of "if". If you see 좋겠다, it is a combination of 좋다 and -겠-. As you can see through the explanation above, -겠- in -(으)면 좋겠다 is used for expressing your assumption. So -(으)면 좋겠다 takes the meaning of "It would be nice if..." or "I would like it if..." and can be also used when you want to say "I hope..." or "I wish...".

⌛ Translation Practice

Translate the English sentences to Korean, and the Korean sentences to English, using the expression that you learned from Key Expression.

1. 월급 오르면 좋겠다!

2. 빨리 토요일이 되면 좋겠다!

3. It would be great if the weather gets warmer!

4. It would be great if I receive a lot of birthday gifts!

42

나랑 사귀었던 사람이야.

He is the one that I used to have a relationship with.

After you study this chapter, you will be able to talk about the things you had done in the past.

Track 42

Tip

This whole conversation is in casual language.

⧖ **Today's Conversation**

A 방금 너랑 얘기한 남자 진짜 잘생겼다.
나 소개해 주면 안 돼?

B 저 사람? 안 돼.

A 아, 왜! 소개해 주면 밥 사 줄게.

B ⋯ 나랑 사귀었던 사람이야.

A The guy you just talked with is so handsome. Can you introduce me to him?

B That guy? Nope.

A Ah, come on! I'll buy you a meal if you introduce me to him.

B ... He's the one that I used to have a relationship with.

Vocabulary ⋯⋯⋯⋯⋯⋯⋯⋯⋯⋯⋯⋯⋯⋯⋯⋯⋯⋯⋯⋯⋯⋯⋯⋯⋯⋯⋯⋯⋯⋯⋯⋯⋯

방금 just now / 너 you / 얘기하다 to talk / 남자 guy, boy / 진짜 really, so much / 잘생기다 to be handsome / 나 I / 소개하다 to introduce / 안 not / 되다 to be okay / 저 that / 사람 person / 아 ah / 왜 why / 밥 meal / 사다 to buy / 사귀다 to make a relationship

⧖ **Listening & Speaking Practice**

Listen carefully! Listen to the whole conversation.
Listen and repeat! Listen to each sentence one by one and repeat.
Let's role-play! Role play with the conversation.

⌛ Key Expression

내가 ˙ 았/었/였던 이야.

It's the [noun] _____ that I used to [verb or phrase] _____.

- 일하다　　　to work at
- 살다　　　　to live in
- 다니다　　　to attend
- 좋아하다　　to like

- 회사　　　company
- 동네　　　neighborhood
- 학교　　　school
- 음식　　　food

Grammar Focus

· The meaning and conjugation of -았/었/였던

When you add -았/었/였던 at the end of a verb stem, it expresses that you "used to" do or be something. -았/었/였 던 implies that the past action or state did not continue or has been completed. You can just put -았/었/였던 after the verb stem, you can use this with action verbs and descriptive verbs also. You should decide how to conjugate them depending on the last letter of the verb stem, the same way you conjugate -아/어/여.

- Verb stems ending in vowels ㅏ or ㅗ + -았던
- Verb stems ending in other vowels + -었던
- Verb stems ending with 하 + 였던 (It is normally be shortened as 했던.)

⌛ Translation Practice

Translate the English sentences to Korean, and the Korean sentences to English, using the expression that you learned from Key Expression.

1. 내가 일했던 회사야.

2. It's the neighborhood that I used to live in.

3. 내가 다녔던 학교야.

4. It's the food that I used to like.

나 내일부터 엄마랑 운동하기로 했어.

I decided to exercise with my mom starting tomorrow.

After you study this chapter, you will be able to talk about what you decided to do.

Track 43

⏳ Today's Conversation

A 나 내일부터 엄마랑 운동하기로 했어.

B 이번에는 진짜 운동할 거야?

A 응, 건강을 위해서 꼭 할 거야.

B 그래. 응원할게.

A I decided to exercise with my mom starting tomorrow.

B Will you exercise for real this time?

A Yeah, I'm definitely going to do it for my health.

B Okay. I'm cheering for you.

Vocabulary

나 I / 내일 tomorrow / 부터 from / 엄마 mom / 운동하다 to exercise / 이번 this time / 진짜 for real / 응 yes / 건강 health / 위하다 to do for / 꼭 surely / 그래 okay / 응원하다 to cheer

⏳ Listening & Speaking Practice

Listen carefully! Listen to the whole conversation.
Listen and repeat! Listen to each sentence one by one and repeat.
Let's role-play! Role play with the conversation.

나 •
　　　　　　　　　　　　　기로 했어.

I decided to _____.

- 서울에 살다　　　　　　to live in Seoul
- 아르바이트(를) 하다　　to work a part-time job
- 술(을) 안 마시다　　　　to not drink alcohol
- 밤에 일찍 자다　　　　　to sleep early at night

Grammar Focus

- **How to change a verb to its noun form**

  There are a few ways to change a verb to its noun form, you can use -기 as a verb ending for it. For example, if you put -기 after the verb stem of 운동하다 which means "to exercise", it will be 운동하기 which means "exercising".

- **The meaning of -기로 하다**

  If you see the structure of -기로 하다, there is -기 to change a verb to its noun form. Then -로 is added, which represents a method or direction. -(으)로 also can be used in situations where you are talking about a choice you are making. So if you say -기로 하다, it has a meaning of you decide to do something from now on.

⌛ Translation Practice

Translate the English sentences to Korean, and the Korean sentences to English, using the expression that you learned from Key Expression.

1. 나 서울에 살기로 했어.

2. I decided to work a part-time job.

3. I decided to not drink alcohol.

4. 나 밤에 일찍 자기로 했어.

전에 허리 치료 받은 적 있어요?

Have you ever received treatment for your back before?

After you study this chapter, you will be able to talk about your own experience.

Track 44

⌛ Today's Conversation

A 어디가 안 좋아서 왔어요?

B 저 허리가 아파서 왔어요.

A 전에 허리 치료 받은 적 있어요?

B 아니요, 이번이 처음이에요.

A What brings you here today?

B I came here because of pain in my waist.

A Have you ever received treatment for your back before?

B No, this is my first time.

Vocabulary

어디 where / 안 not / 좋다 to be good / 오다 to come / 저 [humble] I / 허리 waist / 아프다 to be hurt, to be sick / 전 before / 치료받다 to get treatment / 있다 to exist, to be / 아니 no / 이번 this time / 처음 first time

⌛ Listening & Speaking Practice

Listen carefully! Listen to the whole conversation.
Listen and repeat! Listen to each sentence one by one and repeat.
Let's role-play! Role play with the conversation.

•

(으)ㄴ 적 있어요?

Have you ever [done] _____ ?

- 수술받다   to get surgery
- 병원에 입원하다   to be hospitalized
- 여자 친구랑 싸우다   to argue with your girlfriend
- 그 남자(를) 만나다   to meet that guy

Grammar Focus

• Conjugation of -(으)ㄴ 적 있어요

If you see the structure of -(으)ㄴ 적 있어요, you can see -(으)ㄴ 적 first. 적 means "the time already past", so -(으)ㄴ 적 can be used as "the time that you had done something in the past" with the verb stem. You can use this to talk about your own experience or ask other people about their own. You should decide how to conjugate them depending on the last letter of the verb stem.

- Verb stems ending with a vowel → -ㄴ 적
- Verb stems ending with a consonant → -은 적

⧗ Translation Practice

Translate the English sentences to Korean, and the Korean sentences to English, using the expression that you learned from Key Expression.

1. 수술받은 적 있어요?

2. Have you ever been hospitalized?

3. 여자 친구랑 싸운 적 있어요?

4. Have you ever met that guy?

STUDY DATE :   /

경은 씨 어디 있는지 알아요?

Do you know where Kyeong-eun is?

After you study this chapter, you will be able to ask others if they know about something in detail.

Track 45

⏳ Today's Conversation

> **A** 경은 씨 어디 있는지 알아요?

> **B** 몰라요. 전화해 볼까요?

> **A** 제가 해 봤는데 전화 안 받아요.

> **B** 아, 오늘 경은 씨 휴가인 것 같은데요?

A Do you know where Kyeong-eun is?

B I don't know. Should I try to call her?

A I called her and she didn't answer.

B Ah, it seems like today is her day-off.

Vocabulary

씨 Mr., Mrs., Ms. / 어디 where / 있다 to exist, to be / 알다 to know / 모르다 to not know / 전화하다 to call / 제(저) [humble] I / 안 not / 받다 to get (the phone call), to receive / 아 ah / 오늘 today / 휴가 vacation, day-off

⏳ Listening & Speaking Practice

Listen carefully! Listen to the whole conversation.
Listen and repeat! Listen to each sentence one by one and repeat.
Let's role-play! Role play with the conversation.

•

(으)ㄴ/는지 알아요?

Do you know (what/which/where/when/who/how) _____?

• 누가 제일 똑똑하다   who is the smartest
• 사람(이) 왜 많다   why there are so many people
• 빵(을) 어떻게 만들다   how to make bread
• 영화(가) 언제 시작하다   when the movie starts

Grammar Focus

• **The meaning of -아/어/여 보다**

-아/어/여 보다 has meaning of "to try doing something". 보다 means "to see", so the literal translation of -아/어/여 보다 is "to do something and see (what happens)". You should decide how to conjugate them depending on the last letter of the verb stem, the same way you conjugate -아/어/여.

  • Verb stems ending in vowels ㅏ or ㅗ + -아 보다
  • Verb stems ending in other vowels + -어 보다
  • Verb stems ending with 하 + 여 보다 (It is normally shortened as 해 보다.)

• **Conjugation of -(으)ㄴ/는지**

The verb ending -(으)ㄴ/는지 is used with verbs related to knowing, guessing, informing, or thinking, and to express the meaning of "whether" or "if". It is used with words such as 누구(who), 어디(where), 어떻게(how), 왜(why), 언제 (when), 뭐(what) and 얼마나(how + adverb/adjective) to mark the end of a question inside a compound sentence.

  • Descriptive verb stems ending with a vowel + -ㄴ지
  • Descriptive verb stems ending with a consonant + -은지
  • Action verb stems + -는지 (When the verb stem ends with ㄹ, drop the ㄹ and add -는지)

⧗ Translation Practice

Translate the English sentences to Korean, and the Korean sentences to English, using the expression that you learned from Key Expression.

1. 누가 제일 똑똑한지 알아요?

2. Do you know why there are so many people?

3. 빵을 어떻게 만드는지 알아요?

4. Do you know when the movie starts?

Review Quiz

[1~5] Choose the right Korean phrase from the box for the English translation.

- 제가 살았던
- 날씨가 따뜻해지면
- 영화 언제 시작하는지
- 그 남자 만난 적
- 밤에 일찍 자기로

1. It would be great if the weather gets warmer!

_____ 좋겠다!

2. It's the neighborhood that I used to live in.

_____ 동네예요.

3. I decided to sleep early at night.

나 _____ 했어.

4. Have you ever met that guy?

_____ 있어요?

5. Do you know when the movie starts?

_____ 알아요?

6. Choose the word which is **not** related to hospitals.

○ 치료받다   ○ 입원하다   ○ 사귀다   ○ 수술받다

7. Look at the picture and choose the word that matches it.

생일 선물   월급

아르바이트   건강

8. Choose the pair which is **not** matched properly.

서울 - 싸우다   회사 - 일하다   학교 - 다니다   월급 - 오르다

9. According to the English translation, fill in the blank with the Korean words.

I decided to exercise with my mom starting tomorrow.

= 나 내일부터   로 했어.

10. Choose the appropriate phrase for the conversation below.

A: 경은 씨   알아요?

B: 몰라요. 전화 한번 해 볼까요?

허리가 아파서   어디 있는지   제가 좋아하던

너 자는 동안 내가 다 먹었어.

I ate all of it while you were sleeping.

After you study this chapter, you will be able to talk about what you did while another thing happened.

Track 46

Tip

This whole conversation is in casual language.

⌛ Today's Conversation

A 여기 있던 초콜릿 어디 갔어?

B 너 자는 동안 내가 다 먹었어.

A 야, 그거 내가 생일 선물로 받은 거야.

B 그러면 잘 보관했어야지.

A   Where is the chocolate that was here?

B   I ate all of it while you were sleeping.

A   Hey, that's what I got for my birthday gift.

B   Then you should have kept it safe.

Vocabulary

여기 here / 있다 to exist, to be / 초콜릿 chocolate / 어디 where / 가다 to go / 너 you / 자다 to sleep / 동안 during / 나 I / 다 all / 먹다 to eat / 야 hey / 그거 that, the thing / 생일 birthday / 선물 gift / 받다 to receive / 그러면 then / 잘 well / 보관하다 to keep, to store

⌛ Listening & Speaking Practice

Listen carefully! Listen to the whole conversation.
Listen and repeat! Listen to each sentence one by one and repeat.
Let's role-play! Role play with the conversation.

⏳ Key Expression

•

는 동안   았/었/였어.

While I was [doing] _____ , I [did] _____ .

• 쉬다	to get some rest	• 책(을) 읽다	to read a book
• 요리하다	to cook	• 노래(를) 부르다	to sing a song
• 이동하다	to go somewhere	• 낮잠(을) 자다	to take a nap
• 샤워하다	to shower	• 춤(을) 추다	to dance

Grammar Focus

• **The meaning of -는 동안**

You can use -는 동안 as "while" with the action verb or phrase. 동안 basically means "the time between one moment to another moment", so it can be translated as "while" or "during". You can use 동안 just with noun like 30분 동안 which means "for 30 minutes". If you put the verb ending -ㄴ/는 in front of 동안, you can put a phrase in front of it.

• **How to say "You should have done ~"**

If you want to say "You should have done ~" to others, you can use -았/었/였어야지. There are many ways to say it, but this is the most simple and casual way to say it. However, it could sound rude if you use this expression to someone in a higher societal position than you, so just use it in casual situations. You should decide how to conjugate them depending on the last letter of the verb stem.

⏳ Translation Practice

Translate the English sentences to Korean, and the Korean sentences to English, using the expression that you learned from Key Expression.

1. 쉬는 동안 책 읽었어.

2. 요리하는 동안 노래를 불렀어.

3. While I was going somewhere, I took a nap.

4. While I was showering, I danced.

47

피자를 너무 많이 먹었더니 배 아파.

I ate too much pizza and now my stomach hurts.

After you study this chapter, you will be able to tell the reason why something happened.

🎧 Track 47

Tip

This whole conversation is in casual language.

⏳ Today's Conversation

A　피자를 너무 많이 먹었더니 배 아파.

B　아이고… 적당히 먹었어야지.

A　너무 맛있어서 어쩔 수 없었어.

B　다음에는 조금만 먹어.

A　I ate too much pizza and now my stomach hurts.

B　Oh, my... You should have eaten moderately.

A　I couldn't help it because it was so good.

B　Just eat a little bit next time.

Vocabulary

피자 pizza / 너무 too, so / 많이 a lot, much / 먹다 to eat / 배 stomach / 아프다 to be sick / 아이고 oh, my / 적당히 moderately / 맛있다 to be delicious / 어쩌다 to do somehow / 다음 next / 조금 a little bit

⏳ Listening & Speaking Practice

Listen carefully! Listen to the whole conversation.
Listen and repeat! Listen to each sentence one by one and repeat.
Let's role-play! Role play with the conversation.

•

았/었/였더니   아/어/여.

| [did] _____ and now I'm _____ .

- 잠(을) 안 자다   to not sleep
- 밥(을) 안 먹다   to not eat a meal
- 밤(을) 새우다   to stay up all night
- 물(을) 안 마시다   to not drink water

- 졸리다   to be sleepy
- 배고프다   to be hungry
- 피곤하다   to be tired
- 목마르다   to be thirsty

Grammar Focus

• Particle -만

-만 means "only", and it is a particle so it should be the right behind the noun, pronoun or noun form of the verbs. There are many ways to say "only" in Korean, Using -만 is one of the most widely used and basic way of saying "only".

• The meaning of -았/었/였더니

You can use -았/었/였더니 when you describe two things that you experienced or observed, one after the other. The two things that happened can be either the opposite of each other, or just connected to each other in sequence. In this conversation, -았/었/였더니 is used when one thing is the direct result of the other. You should decide how to conjugate them depending on the last letter of the verb stem.

- Verb stems ending in vowels ㅏ or ㅗ + -았더니
- Verb stems ending in other vowels + -었더니
- Verb stems ending with 하 + 였더니 (It is normally be shortened as 했더니.)

⧖ Translation Practice

Translate the English sentences to Korean, and the Korean sentences to English, using the expression that you learned from Key Expression.

1. 잠을 안 잤더니 졸려.

2. I didn't eat a meal and now I'm hungry.

3. I stayed up all night and now I'm tired.

4. 물을 안 마셨더니 목말라.

48

STUDY DATE :   /

집에서 나오자마자 머리에 새똥 맞았어.

As soon as I came out from home, I got bird poop on my head.

After you study this chapter, you will be able to talk about the thing happening right after something else happened.

Track 48

Tip

This whole conversation is in casual language.

⏳ Today's Conversation

A 아, 아침부터 기분 너무 안 좋아.

B 왜? 무슨 일 있었어?

A 집에서 나오자마자 머리에 새똥 맞았어. 그래서 다시 들어가서 샤워했어.

B 와… 진짜 짜증 났겠다.

A Ah, I've been in a bad mood since this morning.

B Why? What was the matter?

A As soon as I came out from home, I got bird poop on my head. So I went back home and showered.

B Wow... It must have been so annoying.

Vocabulary

아 ah / 아침 morning / 기분 feeling / 너무 too much / 안 not / 좋다 to be good / 왜 why / 무슨 what kind of / 일 thing, matter / 있다 to exist, to be / 집 house / 나오다 to come out / 머리 head / 새똥 bird poop / 맞다 to be hit / 그래서 so / 다시 again / 들어가다 to go into / 샤워하다 to shower / 와 wow / 진짜 really / 짜증나다 to be annoyed

⏳ Listening & Speaking Practice

Listen carefully! Listen to the whole conversation.
Listen and repeat! Listen to each sentence one by one and repeat.
Let's role-play! Role play with the conversation.

•

자마자 았/었/였어.

As soon as I [did] _____, I [did] _____.

• 집에 들어가다	to go into the house	다시 나오다	to come out again
• 자리에 앉다	to sit on the seat	공부하다	to study
• 침대에 눕다	to lie down on the bed	잠이 들다	to fall asleep
• 졸업하다	to graduate	취직하다	to get a job

Grammar Focus

· Conjugation of -자마자

-자마자 means "as soon as (you do something)" or "right after (doing something)" and you can use it with the verb or phrase in front of it. You should put -자마자 after the verb stem, then you can say "as soon as I have done something". Even though the first action happened in the past, you don't need to put it in the past tense, just as a verb stem. And then you can put the second phrase after -자마자 so the sentence can be completed.

⧗ Translation Practice

Translate the English sentences to Korean, and the Korean sentences to English, using the expression that you learned from Key Expression.

1. 집에 들어가자마자 다시 나왔어.

2. As soon as I sat on the seat, I studied.

3. 침대에 눕자마자 잠이 들었어.

4. As soon as I graduated, I got a job.

49

내가 사 줄 테니까 그냥 나와.

I'll buy it for you, so just come out.

After you study this chapter, you will be able to ask others to do something when you offer something else.

Track 49

Tip

This whole conversation is in casual language.

⏳ Today's Conversation

A 오늘 저녁에 뭐 해? 같이 밥 먹자.

B 나 이번 달에 돈이 없어. 다음 달에 만나자.

A 야, 내가 사 줄 테니까 그냥 나와.

B 오케이! 그럼 소고기 사 줘.

A What will you do this evening? Let's have a meal together.

B I don't have money this month. Let's meet next month.

A Hey, I'll buy it for you, so just come out.

B Okay! Then buy me some beef.

Vocabulary

오늘 today / 저녁 evening / 뭐 what / 하다 to do / 같이 together / 밥 meal / 먹다 to eat / 나 I / 이번 this time / 달 month / 돈 money / 없다 to not exist, to not have / 다음 next / 만나다 to meet / 야 hey / 사다 to buy / 그냥 just / 나오다 to come out / 오케이 okay / 그럼 then / 소고기 beef

⏳ Listening & Speaking Practice

Listen carefully! Listen to the whole conversation.
Listen and repeat! Listen to each sentence one by one and repeat.
Let's role-play! Role play with the conversation.

내가 ˙ (으)ㄹ 테니까 너는 ˙ 아/어/여.

I'll _____, so (in return) you _____.

˙ 요리하다	to cook	˙ 설거지하다	to do the dishes
˙ 빨래하다	to do the laundry	˙ 방(을) 청소하다	to clean the room
˙ 다 하다	to do everything	˙ 쉬다	to get some rest
˙ 밥(을) 사다	to pay for the meal	˙ 커피(를) 사다	to pay for the coffee

Grammar Focus

• **The meaning of -(으)ㄹ 테니까**

You can use this structure when you offer to do one thing, and ask the listener to do something else in return. What you ask of the other person does not always have to be a favor, it can also be something that you want them to do for their own good. Therefore, -(으)ㄹ 테니(까) is often translated as "I will do this, so in return, I want you to do this". You should decide how to conjugate them depending on the last letter of the verb stem.

- Verb stems ending with a vowel → -ㄹ 테니까
- Verb stems ending with a consonant → -을 테니까

⏳ Translation Practice

Translate the English sentences to Korean, and the Korean sentences to English, using the expression that you learned from Key Expression.

1. 내가 요리할 테니까 너는 설거지해.

2. I'll do the laundry, so you clean the room.

3. I'll do everything, so you get some rest.

4. 내가 밥을 살 테니까 너는 커피를 사.

한국어 배운 지 얼마나 됐어요?
How long have you studied Korean?

After you study this chapter, you will be able to talk about how long you have done something.

Track 50

Tip

Korean speakers often use 그래? or 그래요? as "Is that so?", to express they are surprised.

⌛ Today's Conversation

A 한국어 배운 지 얼마나 됐어요?

B 6개월 됐어요. 저 혼자 공부했어요.

A 그래요? 6개월밖에 안 됐는데 한국어 정말 잘하시네요.

B 고마워요. 열심히 연습했어요.

A How long have you studied Korean?

B It's been six months. I studied by myself.

A Oh, yeah? It's been just six months and you are really good at Korean.

B Thank you. I practiced hard.

Vocabulary

한국어 Korean language / 배우다 to learn / 얼마 how long / 되다 to have been / 개월 month / 저 [humble] I / 혼자 alone, by oneself / 공부하다 to study / 그래? Is that so? / 안 not / 정말 really / 잘하다 to be good at / 고맙다 to be thankful / 열심히 hard / 연습하다 to practice

⌛ Listening & Speaking Practice

Listen carefully! Listen to the whole conversation.
Listen and repeat! Listen to each sentence one by one and repeat.
Let's role-play! Role play with the conversation.

•

(으)ㄴ 지 얼마나 됐어요?

How long have you [done] _____? / How long has it been since you [did] _____ ?

- 도착하다   to arrive
- 한국에 살다   to live in Korea
- 운동(을) 시작하다   to start to work out
- 이 회사에서 일하다   to work for this company

Grammar Focus

· **The meaning of -(으)ㄴ 지**

-(으)ㄴ 지 is used to indicate that a certain time has passed since a certain act mentioned in the preceding statement is done. After -(으)ㄴ 지, you can usually use past tense as it is usually used to mean that time has already passed. You should decide how to conjugate them depending on the last letter of the verb stem.

- Verb stems ending with a vowel → -ㄴ 지
- Verb stems ending with a consonant → -은 지

⌛ Translation Practice

Translate the English sentences to Korean, and the Korean sentences to English, using the expression that you learned from Key Expression.

1. 도착한 지 얼마나 됐어요?

2. How long have you lived in Korea?

3. 운동 시작한 지 얼마나 됐어요?

4. How long have you worked for this company?

Review Quiz

[1~5] Choose the right Korean phrase from the box for the English translation.

> • 샤워하는 동안   • 침대에 눕자마자   • 내가 빨래할 테니까
>
> • 밤을 새웠더니   • 한국에 산 지

1. While I was showering, I danced.

_____ 춤을 췄어요.

2. I stayed up all night and now I'm tired.

_____ 피곤해.

3. As soon as I lay down on the bed, I fell asleep.

_____ 잠이 들었어요.

4. I'll do the laundry, so you clean the room.

_____ 너는 방 청소해.

5. How long have you lived in Korea?

_____ 얼마나 됐어요?

6. Look at the picture and choose the word that matches it.

○ 빨래하다   ○ 청소하다

○ 설거지하다   ○ 요리하다

7. Choose the pair of words which is **not** properly matched with its translation.

졸리다 - to be sleepy   배고프다 - to be happy

피곤하다 - to be tired   목마르다 - to be thirsty

8. According to the English translation, fill in the blank with the Korean words.

I'll pay for the meal, so you pay for the coffee.

= 내가 _____ 너는 커피 사.

9. Choose the pair which is matched properly.

책 - 자다   노래 - 부르다   낮잠 - 추다   춤 - 읽다

10. Choose the appropriate answer for the question below.

A: 여기 있던 초콜릿 어디 갔어?

B: _____ 내가 다 먹었어.

너 자는 동안   잠을 안 잤더니   내가 사 줄 테니까

Day 01 | Translation Practice

1. I'm a student.

2. 저는 회사원이에요.

3. I'm a teacher.

4. 저는 천재예요.

Day 02 | Translation Practice

1. 저(는) 한국 사람(이) 아니에요.

2. 저(는) 연예인(이) 아니에요.

3. I'm not a teenager.

4. I'm not a fool.

Day 03 | Translation Practice

1. 이름이 뭐예요?

2. 직업이 뭐예요?

3. What is (your) major?

4. What is (your) hobby?

Day 04 | Translation Practice

1. I go to school. / I'm going to school.

2. 저(는) 강의실(에) 가요.

3. I go to the office. / I'm going to the office.

4. 저(는) 편의점(에) 가요.

Day 05 | Translation Practice

1. (저는) 영화(를) 보아요. / (저는) 영화(를) 봐요.

2. (저는) 밥(을) 먹어요.

3. I drink water. / I'm drinking water.

4. I write a letter. / I'm writing a letter.

01-05 | Review Quiz

1. 학생

2. 한국 사람

3. 이름

4. 편의점

5. 물

6. 떡볶이, 김밥

7. 천재 - 바보, 학생 - 선생님

8. 읽어요

9. 실

10. 편지 - 먹다

Day 06 | Translation Practice

1. 저(는) 열일곱 살이에요.
2. 저(는) 스물세 살이에요.
3. I'm thirty-two years old.
4. I'm thirty-nine years old.

Day 07 | Translation Practice

1. Today is March 1st.
2. 오늘(은) 오월 팔 일이에요.
3. 오늘(은) 팔월 십오 일이에요.
4. Today is December 31st.

Day 08 | Translation Practice

1. When is the test?
2. 결혼식이 언제예요?
3. 휴가가 언제예요?
4. 월급날이 언제예요?

Day 09 | Translation Practice

1. 한 시 일 분이에요.
2. 세 시 십 분이에요.
3. 다섯 시 이십오 분이에요.
4. It's 8:59.

Day 10 | Translation Practice

1. That one is 4,500 won.
2. 그거(는) 삼만 삼천 원이에요.
3. 그거(는) 십사만 구천 원이에요.
4. That one is 3,000,000 won.

06-10 | Review Quiz

1. 열일곱
2. 삼월 일 일
3. 월급날
4. 세 시 십 분
5. 사천오백
6. 서른 - 삼십 / 다섯 - 오 / 여덟 - 팔
7. 다섯, 이십오
8. 생일
9. 월요일
10. 여덟 시요.

Day 11 | Translation Practice

1. In the library, I study.
2. In the cafe, I go on a date.
3. 사무실에서 일(을) 해요.
4. 공원에서 산책(을) 해요.

Day 12 | Translation Practice

1. 우리 같이 운동할까요?
2. Shall we take a walk together?
3. 우리 같이 영화(를) 볼까요?
4. Shall we drink coffee together?

Day 13 | Translation Practice

1. 집에 갈래요?
2. Do you want to get some rest at home?
3. 빵(을) 먹을래요?
4. Do you want to take a taxi?

Day 14 | Translation Practice

1. Let's go on a trip.
2. 우리 이사하자.
3. 우리 사귀자.
4. Let's break up.

Day 15 | Translation Practice

1. Is there any tissue here?
2. 여기 비누(가) 있어요?
3. 여기 치약(이) 있어요?
4. Is there a towel here?

11-15 | Review Quiz

1. 도서관
2. 커피
3. 택시
4. 여행
5. 휴지
6. 치킨, 맥주
7. 일(을) 해요
8. 수건, 치약
9. 없어요
10. 안 마실래요.

Day 16 | Translation Practice

1. Can you swim?

2. Can you drive?

3. 한글(을) 읽을 수 있어요?

4. 떡볶이(를) 만들 수 있어요?

Day 17 | Translation Practice

1. I'm doing homework.

2. 집(을) 청소하고 있어요.

3. I'm listening to music.

4. 사진(을) 찍고 있어요.

Day 18 | Translation Practice

1. Is it that you work in Seoul?

2. 매일 운동하는 거예요?

3. 지금 점심(을) 먹는 거예요?

4. Is it that you study by yourself?

Day 19 | Translation Practice

1. 저는 예쁜 사람을 좋아해요.

2. I like people who are kind.

3. 저는 노래(를) 잘하는 사람을 좋아해요.

4. I like people who are good at cooking.

Day 20 | Translation Practice

1. (제가) 싫어하는 옷이에요.

2. (제가) 자주 먹는 음식이에요.

3. This is the song that I listen to every day.

4. (제가) 가끔 가는 식당이에요.

16-20 | Review Quiz

1. 운전

2. 사진

3. 점심

4. 요리

5. 식당

6. 수영하다

7. 자주 - often, 지금 - now

8. 자주 먹는 음식

9. 가끔 가는

10. 노래 듣는 거

Day 21 | Translation Practice

1. 저 옷(을) 사러 가요.

2. I'll go attend class.

3. 저 치료(를) 받으러 가요.

4. I'll go take a walk with the dog.

Day 22 | Translation Practice

1. I'll clean the restroom.

2. 한국어(를) 연습할 거예요.

3. 청바지(를) 입을 거예요.

4. I'll take a bus.

Day 23 | Translation Practice

1. 먼저 퇴근할게요.

2. I'll call you back.

3. I'll wait at home.

4. 내일 아침에 일찍 올게요.

Day 24 | Translation Practice

1. These are the clothes that I'll wear tomorrow.

2. 저녁에 마실 와인이에요.

3. 1년 동안 살 집이에요.

4. This is the gift that I'll bring to Korea.

Day 25 | Translation Practice

1. 어제 김밥(을) 만들었어?

2. Did you go and come back from school today?

3. Did you meet a friend on Friday?

4. 주말에 여행(을) 갔었어?

21-25 | Review Quiz

1. 치료

2. 연습

3. 전화

4. 집

5. 금요일

6. 옷, 청바지

7. 강아지랑 산책

8. 내일 입을

9. 어제 - 해요, 내일 - 했어요

10. 영화 보러 가요.

Day 26 | Translation Practice

1. 여행하려고 왔어요.

2. I came here to learn English.

3. 계좌(를) 만들려고 왔어요.

4. I came here to buy a concert ticket.

Day 27 | Translation Practice

1. Isn't it the fruit that mom sent?

2. 그거 아빠가 준 돈 아니야?

3. Isn't it the rice cake that grandma made?

4. 그거 내가 쓴 편지 아니야?

Day 28 | Translation Practice

1. 물(을) 많이 마시는 거 어때요?

2. 사탕(을) 그만 먹는 거 어때요?

3. How about turning off the cell phone?

4. How about asking the manager?

Day 29 | Translation Practice

1. Please open the door.

2. Please take some pictures for me.

3. 다시 전화해 주세요.

4. 편지(를) 써 주세요.

Day 30 | Translation Practice

1. The dog is big but cute.

2. 방이 깨끗한데 싸요.

3. There are lots of people but there is little food.

4. 가방은 작은데 책은 커요.

26-30 | Review Quiz

1. 계좌 만들려고

2. 엄마가 보낸

3. 사탕을 그만 먹는

4. 사진 좀 찍어

5. 사람은 많은데

6. 영어

7. 가방은 작은데

8. 사진 - 만들다, 펜 – 마시다

9. 다시 전화해

10. 한국어 공부하려고

Day 31 | Translation Practice

1. Don't touch.
2. 마시지 마세요.
3. 들어가지 마세요.
4. Don't take it.

Day 32 | Translation Practice

1. 집에서 나가고 싶어.
2. I want to watch this movie again.
3. 남자 친구(를) 사귀고 싶어.
4. 맛있는 음식(을) 먹고 싶어.

Day 33 | Translation Practice

1. I know how to write Hangeul.
2. 피아노(를) 칠 줄 알아요.
3. I know how to cook bulgogi.
4. 세탁기(를) 사용할 줄 알아요.

Day 34 | Translation Practice

1. Is it okay if I go home early?
2. 카페에 강아지(를) 데려가도 돼요?
3. Is it okay if I listen to music in the room?
4. 영화관에서 햄버거(를) 먹어도 돼요?

Day 35 | Translation Practice

1. It seems like he/she is a good person.
2. It seems like the taste is okay.
3. 불이 너무 밝은 것 같아요.
4. 날씨가 조금 추운 것 같아요.

31-35 | Review Quiz

1. 들어가지
2. 남자 친구 사귀고
3. 불고기 만들 줄
4. 집에 일찍 가도
5. 날씨가 조금 추운
6. 덥다 - 바다, 좋다 - 괜찮다
7. 피아노(를) 칠
8. 한글 - 밝다
9. 데려가
10. 보통 키인 것 같아요.

Day 36 | Translation Practice

1. You should get on the flight at 8 o'clock.

2. 1시까지 사무실에 들어가야 돼요.

3. 12시에 출발해야 돼요.

4. You should work until 6 o'clock.

Day 37 | Translation Practice

1. It's because I'm sleepy.

2. 엄마가 바빠서 그래.

3. 아빠가 배고파서 그래.

4. It's because the dog is bored.

Day 38 | Translation Practice

1. 길(이) 미끄러우니까 조심하세요.

2. 가방(이) 무거우니까 조심하세요.

3. There are many people, so be careful.

4. The car is coming behind you, so be careful.

Day 39 | Translation Practice

1. I was going to school and then picked up the money.

2. I was sleeping and then had a dream.

3. 길을 건너다가 친구를 만났어요.

4. 통화하다가 잠이 들었어요.

Day 40 | Translation Practice

1. You can come by 9 A.M.

2. 서류(를) 제출하면 돼요.

3. You can put the bag here.

4. 휴지(를) 거기서 가져가면 돼요.

36-40 | Review Quiz

1. 사무실에 들어가야

2. 엄마가 바빠서

3. 뒤에 차 오니까

4. 학교에 가다가

5. 가방 여기에 두면

6. 배 - 많다

7. 그릇

8. 들어가다

9. 통화하다가

10. 어제 뛰다가 넘어졌어요.

Day 41 | Translation Practice

1. It would be great if I get a raise at work!

2. It would be great if Saturday comes quickly!

3. 날씨(가) 따뜻해지면 좋겠다!

4. 생일 선물(을) 많이 받으면 좋겠다!

Day 42 | Translation Practice

1. It's the company that I used to work at.

2. 내가 살았던 동네야.

3. It's the school that I used to attend.

4. 내가 좋아했던 음식이야.

Day 43 | Translation Practice

1. I decided to live in Seoul.

2. 나 아르바이트(를) 하기로 했어.

3. 나 술(을) 안 마시기로 했어.

4. I decided to sleep early at night.

Day 44 | Translation Practice

1. Have you ever gotten surgery?

2. 병원에 입원한 적 있어요?

3. Have you ever argued with your girlfriend?

4. 그 남자(를) 만난 적 있어요?

Day 45 | Translation Practice

1. Do you know who is the smartest?

2. 사람(이) 왜 많은지 알아요?

3. Do you know how to make bread?

4. 영화(가) 언제 시작하는지 알아요?

41-45 | Review Quiz

1. 날씨가 따뜻해지면

2. 제가 살았던

3. 밤에 일찍 자기로

4. 그 남자 만난 적

5. 영화 언제 시작하는지

6. 사귀다

7. 생일 선물

8. 서울 - 싸우다

9. 엄마랑 운동하기

10. 어디 있는지

Day 46 | Translation Practice

1. While I was getting some rest, I read a book.
2. While I was cooking, I sang a song.
3. 이동하는 동안 낮잠(을) 잤어.
4. 샤워하는 동안 춤(을) 췄어/추었어.

Day 47 | Translation Practice

1. I didn't sleep and now I'm sleepy.
2. 밥(을) 안 먹었더니 배고파.
3. 밤(을) 새웠더니 피곤해.
4. I didn't drink water and now I'm thirsty.

Day 48 | Translation Practice

1. As soon as I went into the house, I came out again.
2. 자리에 앉자마자 공부했어.
3. As soon as I lay down on the bed, I fell asleep.
4. 졸업하자마자 취직했어.

Day 49 | Translation Practice

1. I'll cook, so you do the dishes.
2. 내가 빨래할 테니까 너는 방(을) 청소해.
3. 내가 다 할 테니까 너는 쉬어.
4. I'll pay for the meal, so you pay for the coffee.

Day 50 | Translation Practice

1. How long has it been since you arrived?
2. 한국에 산 지 얼마나 됐어요?
3. How long has it been since you started to work out?
4. 이 회사에서 일한 지 얼마나 됐어요?

46-50 | Review Quiz

1. 샤워하는 동안
2. 밤을 새웠더니
3. 침대에 눕자마자
4. 내가 빨래할 테니까
5. 한국에 산 지
6. 설거지하다
7. 배고프다 - to be happy
8. 밥(을) 살 테니까
9. 노래 - 부르다
10. 너 자는 동안

How to Say Numbers

Native-Korean Number System

1	하나	[ha-na]	11	열하나	[yeol-ha-na]	30	서른	[seo-reun]
2	둘	[dul]	12	열둘	[yeol-dul]	40	마흔	[ma-heun]
3	셋	[set]	13	열셋	[yeol-set]	50	쉰	[swin]
4	넷	[net]	14	열넷	[yeol-net]	60	예순	[ye-sun]
5	다섯	[da-seot]	15	열다섯	[yeol-da-seot]	70	일흔	[il-heun]
6	여섯	[yeo-seot]	16	열여섯	[yeol-yeo-seot]	80	여든	[yeo-deun]
7	일곱	[il-gop]	17	열일곱	[yeol-il-gop]	90	아흔	[a-heun]
8	여덟	[yeo-deol]	18	열여덟	[yeol-yeo-deol]			
9	아홉	[a-hop]	19	열아홉	[yeol-a-hop]			
10	열	[yeol]	20	스물	[seu-mul]			

Sino-Korean Number System

0	공/영	[gong]/[yeong]						
1	일	[il]	11	십일	[si-bil]	30	삼십	[sam-sip]
2	이	[i]	12	십이	[si-bi]	40	사십	[sa-sip]
3	삼	[sam]	13	십삼	[sip-ssam]	50	오십	[o-sip]
4	사	[sa]	14	십사	[sip-ssa]	60	육십	[yuk-ssip]
5	오	[o]	15	십오	[si-bo]	70	칠십	[chil-sip]
6	육	[yuk]	16	십육	[sim-nyuk]	80	팔십	[pal-sip]
7	칠	[chil]	17	십칠	[sip-chil]	90	구십	[gu-sip]
8	팔	[pal]	18	십팔	[sip-pal]			
9	구	[gu]	19	십구	[sip-kku]			
10	십	[sip]	20	이십	[i-sip]			

100	백	[baek]	100,000	십만	[sim-man]
1,000	천	[cheon]	1,000,000	백만	[baeng-man]
10,000	만	[man]	10,000,000	천만	[cheon-man]

• If you know how to count up to 10, you can combine the numbers to form bigger numbers, starting with 11.

ex)
11 = 10 + 1 = 십 + 일 = 십일
321 = 3 x 100 + 2 x 10 + 1 = 삼 x 백 + 이 x 십 + 일 = 삼백이십일
7,654 = 7 x 1,000 + 6 x 100 + 5 x 10 + 4 = 칠 x 천 + 육 x 백 + 오 x 십 + 사 = 칠천육백오십사

• There are words for 100, 1,000, 10,000 in native-Korean number system, but it is not used normally in modern times. So people normally use native-Korean numbers when they talk about the number under 100.

How to Say Time

Hours

1 o'clock	한 시	[han si]		7 o'clock	일곱 시	[il-gop si]
2 o'clock	두 시	[du si]		8 o'clock	여덟 시	[yeo-deol si]
3 o'clock	세 시	[se si]		9 o'clock	아홉 시	[a-hop si]
4 o'clock	네 시	[ne si]		10 o'clock	열 시	[yeol si]
5 o'clock	다섯 시	[da-seot si]		11 o'clock	열한 시	[yeol-han si]
6 o'clock	여섯 시	[yeo-seot si]		12 o'clock	열두 시	[yeol-du si]

Minutes

1 minute	일 분	[il bun]		16 minutes	십육 분	[sim-nyuk bun]
2 minutes	이 분	[i bun]		17 minutes	십칠 분	[sip-chil bun]
3 minutes	삼 분	[sam bun]		18 minutes	십팔 분	[sip-pal bun]
4 minutes	사 분	[sa bun]		19 minutes	십구 분	[sip-kku bun]
5 minutes	오 분	[o bun]		20 minutes	이십 분	[i-sip bun]
6 minutes	육 분	[yuk bun]		21 minutes	이십일 분	[i-si-bil bun]
7 minutes	칠 분	[chil bun]		22 minutes	이십이 분	[i-si-bi bun]
8 minutes	팔 분	[pal bun]		23 minutes	이십삼 분	[i-sip-ssam bun]
9 minutes	구 분	[gu bun]		24 minutes	이십사 분	[i-sip-ssa bun]
10 minutes	십 분	[sip bun]		25 minutes	이십오 분	[i-si-bo bun]
11 minutes	십일 분	[si-bil bun]		26 minutes	이십육 분	[i-sim-nyuk bun]
12 minutes	십이 분	[si-bi bun]		27 minutes	이십칠 분	[i-sip-chil bun]
13 minutes	십삼 분	[sip-ssam bun]		28 minutes	이십팔 분	[i-sip-pal bun]
14 minutes	십사 분	[sip-ssa bun]		29 minutes	이십구 분	[i-sip-kku bun]
15 minutes	십오 분	[si-bo bun]		30 minutes	삼십 분	[sam-sip bun]

31 minutes	삼십일 분	[sam-si-bil bun]	46 minutes	사십육 분	[sa-sim-nyuk bun]
32 minutes	삼십이 분	[sam-si-bi bun]	47 minutes	사십칠 분	[sa-sip-chil bun]
33 minutes	삼십삼 분	[sam-sip-ssam bun]	48 minutes	사십팔 분	[sa-sip-pal bun]
34 minutes	삼십사 분	[sam-sip-ssa bun]	49 minutes	사십구 분	[sa-sip-kku bun]
35 minutes	삼십오 분	[sam-si-bo bun]	50 minutes	오십 분	[o-sip bun]
36 minutes	삼십육 분	[sam-sim-nyuk bun]	51 minutes	오십일 분	[o-si-bil bun]
37 minutes	삼십칠 분	[sam-sip-chil bun]	52 minutes	오십이 분	[o-si-bi bun]
38 minutes	삼십팔 분	[sam-sip-pal bun]	53 minutes	오십삼 분	[o-sip-ssam bun]
39 minutes	삼십구 분	[sam-sip-kku bun]	54 minutes	오십사 분	[o-sip-ssa bun]
40 minutes	사십 분	[sa-sip bun]	55 minutes	오십오 분	[o-si-bo bun]
41 minutes	사십일 분	[sa-si-bil bun]	56 minutes	오십육 분	[o-sim-nyuk bun]
42 minutes	사십이 분	[sa-si-bi bun]	57 minutes	오십칠 분	[o-sip-chil bun]
43 minutes	사십삼 분	[sa-sip-ssam bun]	58 minutes	오십팔 분	[o-sip-pal bun]
44 minutes	사십사 분	[sa-sip-ssa bun]	59 minutes	오십구 분	[o-sip-kku bun]
45 minutes	사십오 분	[sa-si-bo bun]	60 minutes	육십 분	[yuk-ssip bun]

How to Say Date

The Order of Representing the Date in Korean

month		day		day of the week	
	월 [wol]		일 [il]		요일 [yo-il]

ex) Friday, 3rd of July → 7월 3일 금요일

Months

January	1월	[i-rwol]	July	7월	[chi-rwol]
February	2월	[i-wol]	August	8월	[pa-rwol]
March	3월	[sa-mwol]	September	9월	[gu-wol]
April	4월	[sa-wol]	October	10월	[si-wol]
May	5월	[o-wol]	November	11월	[si-bi-rwol]
June	6월	[you-wol]	December	12월	[si-bi-wol]

Days of the Month

1st	1일	[i-ril]	9th	9일	[gu-il]
2nd	2일	[i-il]	10th	10일	[si-bil]
3rd	3일	[sa-mil]	11th	11일	[si-bi-ril]
4th	4일	[sa-il]	12th	12일	[si-bi-il]
5th	5일	[o-il]	13th	13일	[sim-ssa-mil]
6th	6일	[yu-gil]	14th	14일	[sip-ssa-il]
7th	7일	[chi-ril]	15th	15일	[si-bo-il]
8th	8일	[pa-ril]	16th	16일	[sim-nyu-gil]

17th	17일	[sip-chi-ril]	25th	25일	[i-si-bo-il]
18th	18일	[sip-pa-ril]	26th	26일	[i-sim-nyu-gil]
19th	19일	[sip-kku-il]	27th	27일	[i-sip-chi-ril]
20th	20일	[i-si-bil]	28th	28일	[i-sip-pa-ril]
21st	21일	[i-si-bi-ril]	29th	29일	[i-sip-kku-il]
22nd	22일	[i-si-bi-il]	30th	30일	[sam-si-bil]
23rd	23일	[i-sip-ssa-mil]	31st	31일	[sam-si-bi-ril]
24th	24일	[i-sip-ssa-il]			

Days of the Week

Sunday	Monday	Tuesday	Wednesday	Thursday	Friday	Saturday
일요일	월요일	화요일	수요일	목요일	금요일	토요일
[i-ryo-il]	[wo-ryo-il]	[hwa-yo-il]	[su-yo-il]	[mo-gyo-il]	[geu-myo-il]	[to-yo-il]

More Expressions About Dates

the day before yesterday	yesterday	today	tomorrow	the day after tomorrow
그제 or 그저께	어제 or 어저께	오늘	내일	내일모레
[geu-je] [geu-jeo-kke]	[eo-je] [eo-jeo-kke]	[o-neul]	[nae-il]	[nae-il-mo-re]

last week	this week	next week	last month	this month	next month
지난주	이번 주	다음 주	지난달	이번 달	다음 달
[ji-nan-ju]	[i-beon ju]	[da-eum ju]	[ji-nan-dal]	[i-beon dal]	[da-eum dal]

last year	this year	next year
작년	올해	내년
[jang-nyeon]	[ol-hae]	[nae-nyeon]

Glossary

Day 01

안녕하다	to be peaceful
저	[humble] I
반갑다	to be glad to meet
네	yes
제	[humble] my
이름	name
학생	student
회사원	office worker, businessman
선생님	[honorific] teacher
천재	genius

Day 02

씨	Mr., Mrs., Ms.
학생	student
저	[humble] I
아	ah
선생님	[honorific] teacher
아니	no
학부모	parent of a student
한국	Korea, Korean
사람	person, human
연예인	celebrity
청소년	teenager
바보	fool

Day 03

이거	this thing
뭐	what
떡볶이	stir-fried rice cake
한국	Korea, Korean
음식	food
저거	that thing
그거	it, the thing
김밥	seaweed rice roll
이름	name
직업	job, occupation
전공	major (in college)
취미	hobby

Day 04

씨	Mr., Mrs., Ms.
어디	where
가다	to go
저	[humble] I
집	home, house
화장실	restroom
아	ah
파이팅	good luck, go for it
학교	school
강의실	lecture room

사무실	office
편의점	convenience store

Day 05

씨	Mr., Mrs., Ms.
뭐	what
하다	to do
책	book
읽다	to read
그	that
재미있다	to be interesting, to be fun
아니	no
재미없다	to be not interesting, to be not fun
영화	movie
보다	to watch, to see
밥	rice, meal
먹다	to eat
물	water
마시다	to drink
편지	letter
쓰다	to write

Day 06

씨	Mr., Mrs., Ms.

몇	how many
살	age, years
저	[humble] I
스물넷	twenty-four
에이	hmph, pff
거짓말	lie
미안하다	to be sorry
사실	actually, in fact
서른	thirty
열일곱	seventeen
스물셋	twenty-three
서른둘	thirty-two
서른아홉	thirty-nine

Day 07

오늘	today
몇	how many, what number
월	month
며칠	what date
일	day
고맙다	to be thankful
아	ah
무슨	what, what kind of
요일	day of the week
하하	haha

월요일	Monday	시	hour
3월	March	분	minute
5월	May	영화	movie
8월	August	언제	when
12월	December	시작하다	to start
		빨리	quickly
		오다	to come

Day 08

씨	Mr., Mrs., Ms.	하나	one
생일	birthday	일	one
언제	when	셋	three
월	month	십	ten
일	day	다섯	five
제	[humble] my	이십오	twenty-five
안	not	여덟	eight
물어보다	to ask	오십구	fifty-nine
궁금하다	to be curious		
시험	exam, test		

Day 10

결혼식	wedding ceremony	저기	there
휴가	vacation	이	this
월급날	payday	바지	pants
		얼마	how much

Day 09

		만	ten thousand
지금	now	원	won(Korean currency unit)
몇	how many, what number	저	that
		치마	skirt

그거	it, the thing, that (thing)		사무실	office
천	thousand		일	work
사천오백	four thousand five hundred		산책	taking a walk
삼만	thirty thousand			
삼천	three thousand			

Day 12

십사만	one hundred forty thousand		아	ah
구천	nine thousand		너무	too much
삼백만	three million		배고프다	to be hungry
			저	[humble] I

Day 11

우리	we			
씨	Mr., Mrs., Ms.		같이	together
아침	morning		저녁	evening, dinner
뭐	what		먹다	to eat
하다	to do		네	yes
저	[humble] I		뭐	what
요즘	these days		치킨	chicken
운동하다	to exercise		좋다	to be good
운동	exercise		운동하다	to exercise
네	yes		산책하다	to take a walk
한강	Han River		영화	movie
공원	park		보다	to watch, to see
도서관	library		커피	coffee
공부	study		마시다	to drink
카페	cafe			
데이트	date, going on a date			

Day 13

씨	Mr., Mrs., Ms.
맥주	beer
마시다	to drink
저	[humble] I
괜찮다	to be okay
안	not
왜	why
술	alcohol
잘	well
못	cannot
집	home, house
가다	to go
쉬다	to get some rest
빵	bread
먹다	to eat
택시	taxi
타다	to ride, to take (a vehicle)

Day 14

우리	we, us
카페	cafe
가다	to go
그래	okay
뭐	what

마시다	to drink
나	I
카페라떼	cafe latte
그러면	then
아메리카노	americano
여행	trip, travel
이사하다	to move to another house
사귀다	to date, to become a couple
헤어지다	to break up

Day 15

사장	boss
님	[honorific] Mr., Mrs., Ms.
우유	milk
있다	to exist, to be
네	yes
저	that
냉장고	refrigerator
감사하다	to be thankful
혹시	by any chance
케이크	cake
아니	no
없다	to not exist, to not be
휴지	tissue
비누	soap

치약	toothpaste		보다	to watch, to see
수건	towel		자주	often
			네	yes
			거의	almost
			매일	every day

Day 16

한국어	Korean language		과제	homework, project
하다	to do		집	home, house
네	yes		청소하다	to clean
와	wow		노래	song, music
잘하다	to be good at		듣다	to listen
아니	no		사진	photo
조금	a little		찍다	to take (a photo)
못하다	to be not good at			
수영하다	to swim			
운전하다	to drive			
한글	Hangeul (Korean alphabet)			

Day 18

읽다	to read		어	oh
떡볶이	stir-fried rice cake		한국	Korea, Korean
만들다	to make, to cook		노래	song, music
			듣다	to listen
			네	yes

Day 17

지금	now		저	[humble] I
뭐	what		진짜	really
하다	to do		많이	a lot
한국	Korea, Korean		좋아하다	to like
드라마	drama		그런데	but
			춤추다	to dance

더	more
서울	Seoul
일하다	to work
매일	every day
운동하다	to exercise, to work out
지금	now
점심	lunch
먹다	to eat
혼자	alone, by oneself
공부하다	to study

Day 19

씨	Mr., Mrs., Ms.
어떤	which, what kind of
남자	guy
좋아하다	to like
저	[humble] I
잘생기다	to be handsome
사람	person
하하	haha
그리고	and
똑똑하다	to be smart
좋다	to be good
예쁘다	to be pretty
친절하다	to be kind

노래	song, music
잘하다	to be good at
요리	cooking

Day 20

그거	it, the thing
누구(의)	whose
사진	photo
제(저)	[humble] I
제일	the most
좋아하다	to like
가수	singer
우와	wow
사람	person
눈	eye
고양이	cat
같다	to be same, to be like
맞다	to be right, to be correct
그래서	so
이	this
별명	nickname
싫어하다	to hate
옷	clothes
자주	often
먹다	to eat

음식	food	치료	treatment
매일	every day	받다	to get, to receive
듣다	to listen	강아지	dog
노래	song, music	산책하다	to take a walk
가끔	sometimes		
가다	to go		
식당	restaurant		

Day 22

오늘	today
저녁	evening
뭐	what
하다	to do
그냥	just
집	home
쉬다	to get some rest
저	[humble] me
같이	together
한강	Han River
공원	park
가다	to go
오	oh
좋다	to be good
화장실	restroom
청소하다	to clean
한국어	Korean language
연습하다	to practice
청바지	jeans

Day 21

이번	this, this time
주말	weekend
뭐	what
하다	to do
저	[humble] I
남편	husband
영화	movie
보다	to watch, to see
가다	to go
어떤	what kind of, which
아직	yet
모르다	to not know
옷	clothes
사다	to buy
수업	class
듣다	to take (a lesson)

입다	to wear
버스	bus
타다	to ride, to take (a vehicle)

Day 23

저기	there
주문하다	to order
네	yes
뭐	what
드리다	[honorific] to give
삼겹살	pork belly
-인분	serving
된장찌개	soybean paste stew
하나	one
주다	to give
알다	to know, to understand
먼저	first, earlier
퇴근하다	to leave work
다시	again
전화하다	to call (via the phone)
집	home, house
기다리다	to wait
내일	tomorrow
아침	morning
일찍	early

오다	to come

Day 24

와	wow
음식	food
엄청	very
많다	to be a lot of amount
네	yes
오늘	today
점심	lunch
먹다	to eat
아	ah
친구	friend
파티	party
하다	to do
아니	no
저	[humble] I
혼자	alone, by oneself
다	all
내일	tomorrow
입다	to wear
옷	clothes
저녁	evening, dinner
마시다	to drink
와인	wine

년	year		만들다	to make, to cook
동안	during, for		오늘	today
살다	to live		학교	school
집	house		다녀오다	to go and come back
한국	Korea		금요일	Friday
가져가다	to bring		친구	friend
선물	gift		만나다	to meet
			주말	weekend
			여행	trip, travel

Day 25

여보세요	hello (on the phone)
서울역	Seoul Station
도착하다	to arrive
응	yes
방금	just (now)
우리	we
어디서	where
만나다	to meet
번	No. (for numbers)
출구	exit
오다	to come
알다	to know
거기	there
보다	to see, to meet
어제	yesterday
김밥	gimbap

가다	to go

Day 26

어느	which
나라	country
오다	to come
저	[humble] I
프랑스	France
여행하다	to travel
아니	no
한국어	Korean language
공부하다	to study
여행하다	to travel
영어	English
배우다	to learn
계좌	bank account

만들다	to make		돈	money
콘서트	concert		할머니	grandma
티켓	ticket		만들다	to make
사다	to buy		떡	rice cake
			나	I
			쓰다	to write

Day 27

자기	oneself
우리	we
어떤	what kind of, which
영화	movie
보다	to watch
글쎄	well
이	this
어때	how about
그거	it, the thing
아니	not
뭐	what
나	I
안	not
누구	who
엄마	mom
보내다	to send
과일	fruit
아빠	dad
주다	to give

쓰다	to write
편지	letter

Day 28

저	[humble] I
오늘	today
다이어트	diet
시작하다	to start
그런데	but
지금	now
뭐	what
먹다	to eat
이거	this
아이스크림	ice cream
끊다	to stop doing
물	water
많이	a lot
마시다	to drink
사탕	candy
그만	stop

핸드폰	cell phone
끄다	to turn off
팀장	manager
님	[honorific] Mr., Mrs., Ms.
물어보다	to ask

다시	again
전화하다	to call (via the phone)
편지	letter
쓰다	to write

Day 29

씨	Mr., Mrs., Ms.
저	[humble] I
좀	some
도와주다	to give help
뭐	what
돕다	to help
저	that
박스	box
같이	together
들다	to hold, to lift
음	umm
점심	lunch
사다	to buy
그러면	then
문	door
열다	to open
사진	photo, picture
찍다	to take (a photo)

Day 30

씨	Mr., Mrs., Ms.
뭐	what
하다	to do
가방	bag
사다	to buy
인터넷	internet
검색하다	to search
오	oh
이	this
예쁘다	to be pretty
이거	this, this thing
그거	the thing, that
진짜	really
비싸다	to be expensive
만	ten thousand
원	won(Korean currency unit)
강아지	dog
크다	to be big
귀엽다	to be cute

방	room
깨끗하다	to be clean
싸다	to be cheap
사람	person
많다	to be a lot of amount
음식	food
적다	to be of little amount
가방	bag
작다	to be small
책	book
크다	to be big

Day 31

씨	Mr., Mrs., Ms.
이	this
영화	movie
보다	to watch
재미있다	to be interesting
진짜	really
재미없다	to be boring
그래?	Is that so?
추천하다	to recommend
다	all
만지다	to touch
마시다	to drink

들어가다	to go in
가져가다	to take

Day 32

아	ah
너무	so, much
덥다	to be hot
바다	ocean, beach
수영하다	to swim
가다	to go
나	I
같이	together
좋다	to be good
언제	when
이번	this time
주	week
시간	time
안	not
되다	to be able to
다음	next
금요일	Friday
집	home, house
나가다	to go out, to leave
이	this
영화	movie

다시	again		피아노	piano
보다	to watch, to see		치다	to play (instrument)
남자	boy, guy		불고기	bulgogi
친구	friend		만들다	to make, to cook
사귀다	to become a couple		세탁기	washing machine
맛있다	to be delicious		사용하다	to use
음식	food			
먹다	to eat			

Day 34

엄마	mom
저	[humble] I

Day 33

씨	Mr., Mrs., Ms.		친구	friend
자전거	bike		게임하다	to play a game
타다	to ride		되다	to be possible
알다	to know		숙제	homework
네	yes		다	all
저	[humble] I		아니	no
토요일	Saturday		먼저	first
마다	every		숙제하다	to do homework
가다	to go		안	not
같이	together		집	home, house
모르다	to not know		일찍	early
제	[humble] I		가다	to go
가르치다	to teach		카페	cafe
한글	Hangeul (Korean alphabet)		강아지	dog
쓰다	to write		데려가다	to bring

방	room
음악	music
듣다	to listen
영화관	movie theater
햄버거	hamburger
먹다	to eat

Day 35

씨	Mr., Mrs., Ms.
키	height
어떻다	to be how
되다	to be
한국	Korea
크다	to be tall
음	well
제	[humble] my
생각	thinking, opinion
보통	normal
좋다	to be good
사람	person
맛	taste
괜찮다	to be okay
불	light
너무	too much
밝다	to be bright

날씨	weather
조금	little bit
춥다	to be cold

Day 36

사장	boss
님	[honorific] Mr., Mrs., Ms.
지금	now
자리	seat
있다	to exist, to be
없다	to not exist, to be not
좀	a little
기다리다	to wait
얼마	how long
분	minute
정도	around, about
시	hour
비행기	plane
타다	to ride
사무실	office
들어가다	to go into
출발하다	to depart, to start to go
근무하다	to work

Day **37**

방	room
이상하다	to be weird
냄새나다	to smell
나	I
오늘	today
발	foot
안	not
씻다	to wash
미안하다	to be sorry
야	hey
가다	to go
빨리	quickly
토하다	to vomit, to puke
싫다	to dislike
귀찮다	to be annoyed
졸리다	to be sleepy
엄마	mom
바쁘다	to be busy
아빠	dad
배고프다	to be hungry
강아지	dog
심심하다	to be bored

Day **38**

주문하다	to order
음식	food
나오다	to come out
아	ah
여기	here
주다	to give
네	yes, okay
그릇	bowl
뜨겁다	to be hot
조심하다	to be careful
감사하다	to be thankful
길	road
미끄럽다	to be slippery
가방	bag
무겁다	to be heavy
사람	person
엄청	very
많다	to be a lot of amount
뒤	back, behind
차	car
오다	to come

Day **39**

어머	oh

너	you		만나다	to meet
팔	arm		통화하다	to talk over the phone
왜	why		들다	to fall (asleep)
그렇다	to be so			
어제	yesterday			
뛰다	to run			

너	you
팔	arm
왜	why
그렇다	to be so
어제	yesterday
뛰다	to run
넘어지다	to fall down
아이고	oh, my
엄청	very
크다	to be big
멍들다	to get a bruise
네	yes
너무	too much
아프다	to be hurt
학교	school
가다	to go
돈	money
줍다	to pick up (from the floor)
잠	sleep
자다	to sleep
꿈	dream
꾸다	to dream
길	road, street
건너다	to cross (the street)
친구	friend

만나다	to meet
통화하다	to talk over the phone
들다	to fall (asleep)

Day **40**

죄송하다	[humble] to be sorry
여기	here
서울역	Seoul Station
어떻게	how
가다	to go
홍대입구역	Hongik University Station
지하철	subway
타다	to ride
감사하다	to be thankful
버스	bus
있다	to exist, to be
네	yes
그런데	but
더	more
오래	for a long time
걸리다	to take (time)
아침	morning
오다	to come
서류	document
제출하다	to submit

가방	bag		다녀오다	to go and come back
여기	here		내	my
두다	to put		선물	gift
휴지	tissue		사다	to buy
거기	there		오다	to come
가져가다	to take		월급	salary
			오르다	to rise
			빨리	quickly

Day 41

아	ah		토요일	Saturday
빨리	quickly		되다	to become
방학	vacation		날씨	weather
되다	to become		따뜻해지다	to get warmer
좋다	to be good		생일	birthday
이번	this time		선물	gift
무슨	what kind of, any		많이	a lot
계획	plan		받다	to receive
있다	to exist, to be			
응	yes			
나	I			

Day 42

한국	Korea		방금	just now
여행	trip		너	you
가다	to go		얘기하다	to talk
서울	Seoul		남자	guy, boy
제주도	Jeju Island		진짜	really, so much
잘	well		잘생기다	to be handsome
			나	I

소개하다	to introduce		이번	this time
안	not		진짜	for real
되다	to be okay		응	yes
저	that		건강	health
사람	person		위하다	to do for
아	ah		꼭	surely
왜	why		그래	okay
밥	meal		응원하다	to cheer
사다	to buy		서울	Seoul
사귀다	to make a relationship		살다	to live
일하다	to work		아르바이트	part-time job
회사	company		하다	to do
살다	to live		술	alcohol
동네	neighborhood		안	not
다니다	to attend		마시다	to drink
학교	school		밤	night
좋아하다	to like		일찍	early
음식	food		자다	to sleep

Day 43

나	I
내일	tomorrow
부터	from
엄마	mom
운동하다	to exercise

Day 44

어디	where
안	not
좋다	to be good
오다	to come
저	[humble] I

허리	waist	제(저)	[humble] I
아프다	to be hurt, to be sick	안	not
전	before	받다	to get (the phone call), to receive
치료받다	to get treatment	아	ah
있다	to exist, to be	오늘	today
아니	no	휴가	vacation, day-off
이번	this time	누구	who
처음	first time	제일	the most
수술받다	to get surgery	똑똑하다	to be smart
병원	hospital	사람	person
입원하다	to be hospitalized	왜	why
여자	girl	많다	to be a lot of amount
친구	friend	빵	bread
싸우다	to argue, to fight	어떠하다	to be how
그	that	만들다	to make
남자	guy, boy	영화	movie
만나다	to meet	언제	when
		시작하다	to start

Day 45

씨	Mr., Mrs., Ms.
어디	where
있다	to exist, to be
알다	to know
모르다	to not know
전화하다	to call

Day 46

여기	here
있다	to exist, to be
초콜릿	chocolate
어디	where
가다	to go

너	you
자다	to sleep
동안	during
나	I
다	all
먹다	to eat
야	hey
그거	that, the thing
생일	birthday
선물	gift
받다	to receive
그러면	then
잘	well
보관하다	to keep, to store
쉬다	to get some rest
책	book
읽다	to read
요리하다	to cook
노래	song, music
부르다	to sing (a song)
이동하다	to move, to go
낮잠	nap
자다	to sleep
샤워하다	to shower
춤	dance

추다	to dance

Day 47

피자	pizza
너무	too, so
많이	a lot, much
먹다	to eat
배	stomach
아프다	to be sick
아이고	oh, my
적당히	moderately
맛있다	to be delicious
어쩌다	to do somehow
다음	next
조금	a little bit
잠	sleeping
안	not
자다	to sleep
졸리다	to be sleepy
밥	meal
먹다	to eat
배고프다	to be hungry
밤	night
새우다	to stay up (all night)
피곤하다	to be tired

물	water
마시다	to drink
목마르다	to be thirsty

Day 48

아	ah
아침	morning
기분	feeling
너무	too much
안	not
좋다	to be good
왜	why
무슨	what kind of
일	thing, matter
있다	to exist, to be
집	house
나오다	to come out
머리	head
새똥	bird poop
맞다	to be hit
그래서	so
다시	again
들어가다	to go into
샤워하다	to shower
와	wow

진짜	really
짜증나다	to be annoyed
자리	seat
앉다	to sit
공부하다	to study
침대	bed
눕다	to lie down
잠	sleeping
들다	to fall (asleep)
졸업하다	to graduate
취직하다	to get a job

Day 49

오늘	today
저녁	evening
뭐	what
하다	to do
같이	together
밥	meal
먹다	to eat
나	I
이번	this time
달	month
돈	money
없다	to not exist, to not have

다음	next	개월	month
만나다	to meet	저	[humble] I
야	hey	혼자	alone, by oneself
사다	to buy	공부하다	to study
그냥	just	그래?	Is that so?
나오다	to come out	안	not
오케이	okay	정말	really
그럼	then	잘하다	to be good at
소고기	beef	고맙다	to be thankful
요리하다	to cook	열심히	hard
설거지하다	to do the dishes	연습하다	to practice
빨래하다	to do the laundry	도착하다	to arrive
방	room	한국	Korea
청소하다	to clean	살다	to live
다	all	운동	exercise
하다	to do	시작하다	to start
쉬다	to get some rest	이	this
밥	meal	회사	company
커피	coffee	일하다	to work

Day 50

한국어	Korean language
배우다	to learn
얼마	how long
되다	to have been

TTMIK Book Audio App

Download our app TTMIK: Audio to listen to all the
audio and video tracks from our book conveniently on
your phone! The app is available for free on both iOS
and Android. Search for TTMIK: Audio in your app store.